HARCOURT

Math

Involvement
Activities

Grade 2

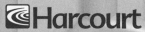

Orlando   Austin   Chicago   New York   Toronto   London   San Diego

Visit *The Learning Site!*
www.harcourtschool.com

CONTENTS

CONTENTS

Using the Family Involvement Activities

The *Family Involvement Activities* provide you with an important means of communicating with family members concerning what their children are learning in mathematics. In addition, these materials provide models that enable parents and other family members to assist students in the learning process.

The *Family Involvement Activities* serve several purposes:

- to provide instructional materials that enable older sibling, parental, or other adult tutoring of new concepts introduced in the student text;
- to provide a home math activity that students can complete with family members;
- to provide practice of new concepts and skills in the form of homework; and
- to provide a concept-based math game for family members to play together.

At the beginning of the year, send home the initial family letter to introduce the *Family Involvement Activities*. At the same time, send the glossary and "Helping Your Child with Standardized Tests" to serve as yearlong references.

As you begin each chapter, use the chapter letter to communicate content and vocabulary; the "Home Activity," "Practice/Homework," and "Math Game" to provide practice with key skills and concepts. To monitor student progress, you might regard the "Practice/Homework" page as a homework assignment to be returned to you for your evaluation.

The use of the *Family Involvement Activities* in conjunction with the student textbook will increase family involvement in student learning and will help each student to achieve optimal success in their study of mathematics.

Name

Date

Dear Family,

Your child has embarked on a new and exciting year in the study of mathematics. Each year previous skills are reinforced and new skills are taught.

In order to provide you with important information about what your child will be learning this year, the second grade Family Involvement letters detail what all second grade students are expected to know and be able to do. Also included is a glossary that contains this year's math terms. Please keep this glossary handy to use as a reference throughout the school year. In addition, a special section titled "Helping Your Child with Standardized Tests" is provided. The section offers tips on how you can assist your child to develop strategies for success on standardized tests.

As your child begins each new chapter in HARCOURT MATH, he or she will bring home a Family Involvement Activity. Each of these activities provides instructional materials that enable older sibling, parental, or other adult tutoring of new concepts introduced in the text. These include a home activity that your child can complete with family members; practice of new concepts in the form of homework; and a concept-based math game for family members to play together.

Remember that you do not have to be a mathematician to participate in your child's mathematics education. Showing your child how mathematics relates to real-world experience is an important part of his or her education—a part in which you are the major contributor.

Sincerely,

Helping Your Child with Standardized Tests

A Little Each Day

With a little time, assistance, and encouragement every day, you can help your child develop strategies that lead to success on his or her school's standardized test. By helping your child study at home over the course of the year, rather than just before the test, you can ease the stress of taking the test and give your child more practice with concepts and skills problems that appear on the test.

Helping with Concepts

Concepts are general ideas that explain the how's and why's of mathematics. They often generate the response, "Oh, now I get it!"

Some test items focus on concepts. Other items focus on skills, such as adding and subtracting. However, if students have forgotten how to find the answer to a skill item, they can often use their understanding of concepts to devise other ways to find the answer.

Word problems often involve both concepts and skills. Students need to understand concepts to decide how to go about solving a problem; for example, whether they should add or subtract. They need to use skills to compute the answer.

To help your child develop an understanding of concepts, ask your child to explain homework problems to you. You might begin by having your child read a problem aloud. Then have your child restate the problem and describe how he or she arrived at the solution.

Concepts Through Vocabulary

Mathematics vocabulary represents major mathematical concepts. Your child needs to understand vocabulary in order to comprehend test items and to communicate answers to test scorers. For example, if a multiple choice item asks your child to find the area of a garden, your child needs to know that *area* is the number of square units that cover the garden's surface, *not* the distance around the garden.

Have your child tell you about the vocabulary words that appear on the family letters. Strive to use the vocabulary words in informal discussions so that your child has practice hearing and using the words. Ask questions that help your child think about the words' meanings. For example: What is the difference between area and perimeter (or A.M. and P.M., or multiplication and addition, or a bar graph and line graph, and so on)? How could we find the area and perimeter of this floor?

Use the glossary to keep track of the vocabulary that your child knows. You might place checkmarks next to the words that the child has studied, and return those words later for review.

Another way to increase your child's vocabulary is to make reading a natural part of his or her routine. Provide a variety of books, magazines, and newspapers for your child to read at home. Read to your child to open topics for discussion, and encourage your child to read to you. At times when you read silently together, discuss what each of you has learned.

Assisting with Skills

While concepts involve *understanding* mathematics, skills involve *doing* mathematics, such as recalling basic facts or following procedures. Just as with sports, mathematics skills improve with practice.

Homework provides important skill practice. To optimize the benefit of homework, find a quiet, comfortable place in your home for your child to do work.

Meet with your child's teacher on a regular basis to discuss his or her progress. Find out what activities can be done at home to help your child's test performance.

Avoiding Mistakes

Mistakes on tests are common and fixable. Some mistakes come from misinterpreting directions and questions. Other mistakes may be computational errors.

Help your child get into the habit of reading directions and questions carefully. Encourage your child to ask questions about any instructions that are unclear. After your child completes a homework exercise, encourage him or her to reread the directions or the questions to make sure that the answer is appropriate.

Students can avoid making computational errors by checking their answers. Many multiple-choice items include responses that are common errors; therefore children should not assume that their computed answers are correct if their answers are among the given answer choices.

Encourage your child to get into the habit of checking homework answers. Your child may either estimate to find out if the answer is reasonable, or use computation to see if the answer is correct. If time is a factor on a standardized test, estimating is the quickest way to check. However, if the numbers in answer choices are about the same, then your child will need to use computation to check.

Building Confidence

By providing support and guidance, you can help your child perform at his or her best on standardized tests. Always be positive and express confidence that your child will do well on the test. Let your child know that all you expect is his or her best effort.

PICTURE GLOSSARY

add (page 73)

To join 2 groups.

addend (page 69)

$$4 + 4 = 8$$

addend

angle (page 319)

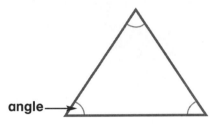

angle→

area (page 433)

The number of units that cover a flat surface.

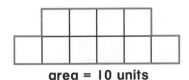

area = 10 units

bar graph (page 59)

Hours of Playing Sports Last Week										
Raven										
Carly										
Jack										
Beth										

0 1 2 3 4 5 6 7 8 9 10
Number of Hours

Children

calendar (page 261)

A **calendar** shows the 12 months of a year in order.

centimeter (page 415)

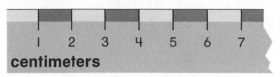

1 2 3 4 5 6 7
centimeters

Used to measure the length of short objects.

certain (page 295)

Green is a **certain** outcome.

change (page 231)

The difference between the price of an item and the money you give the clerk.

circle (page 317)

column addition (page 183)

$$
\begin{array}{r}
1 \\
56 \\
14 \\
+\ 4 \\
\hline
4
\end{array}
$$

>10 >14

In **column addition**, first add the ones. Then add the tens.

concrete graph (page 55)

cone (page 331)

congruent (page 345)

Figures that are the same size and shape are **congruent**.

corner (page 333)

corner →

count back (page 83)

What is 6 − 2?

Say 6.
Count back 2.
5, 4
The difference is 4.

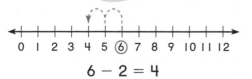

6 − 2 = 4

count on (page 67)

What is 3 + 2?

Say 3.
Count on 2.
4, 5
The sum is 5.

3 + 2 = 5

cube (page 331)

cup (page 401)

cylinder (page 331)

date (page 263)

November						
Sunday	Monday	Tuesday	Wednesday	Thursday	Friday	Saturday
	1	2	3	4	5	6
7	8	9	10	11	12	13
14	15	16	17	18	19	20
21	22	23	24	25	26	27
28	29	30				

The **date** is November 28.

day (page 263)

The **day** is Monday.

November						
Sunday	Monday	Tuesday	Wednesday	Thursday	Friday	Saturday
	1	2	3	4	5	6
7	8	9	10	11	12	13
14	15	16	17	18	19	20
21	22	23	24	25	26	27
28	29	30				

decimal point (page 211)

$1.00

decimal point

difference (page 83)

$6 - 4 = 2$

The **difference** is 2.

digits (page 7)

51

digit ⟶ ⟵ digit

51 has two **digits**.

divide (page 529)

To place into equal groups.

dollar sign (page 211)

$1.00

dollar sign

doubles (page 69)

Both addends are the same in a doubles fact.

$4 + 4 = 8$

doubles plus one (page 69)

One addend is one more in a doubles-plus-one fact.

$4 + 5 = 9$

edge (page 333)

edge ⟶

equal parts (page 445)

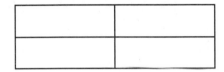

The rectangle has 4 **equal parts**.

equally likely (page 301)

Yellow and blue are **equally likely** to be pulled from the bag.

estimate (page 133)

To find about how many.

even (page 25)

$$0, 2, 4, 6, 8, 10$$

event (page 293)

An outcome is a possible result of an **event**.

face (page 333)

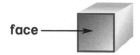

face →

fact family (page 85)

6, 7, and 13 are the numbers in this **fact family**.

$$6 + 7 = 13 \qquad 7 + 6 = 13$$
$$13 - 6 = 7 \qquad 13 - 7 = 6$$

flip (page 349)

foot (page 387)

A sheet of notebook paper is about 1 **foot** long.

1 foot = 12 inches

fraction (page 445)

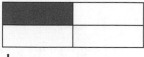

$\frac{1}{4}$ **of the whole is red.**

gallon (page 401)

1 gallon = 4 quarts

gram (page 419)

Used to measure the mass of light objects.

grid (page 281)

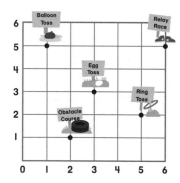

group (page 453)

1 apple
_____
3 pieces of fruit in all

half dollar (page 207)

half-hour (page 247)

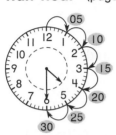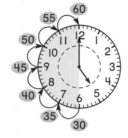

There are 30 minutes in a **half-hour**.

hexagon (page 317)

hour (page 245)

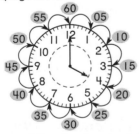

There are 60 minutes in 1 **hour**.

hundreds (page 469)

2 hundreds

impossible (page 295)

Blue is an **impossible** outcome.

inch (page 385)

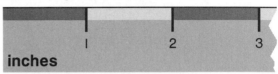

inches

is equal to = (page 37)

25 **is equal to** 25.

25 = 25

is greater than > (page 37)

33 **is greater than** 29.

63 > 29

is less than < (page 37)

29 **is less than** 41.

29 < 63

kilogram (page 419)

Used to measure the mass of heavier objects.

least likely (page 299)

Blue is the **least likely** outcome.

less likely (page 299)

Yellow is a **less likely** outcome.

likely (page 297)

Blue is a **likely** outcome.

line graph (page 283)

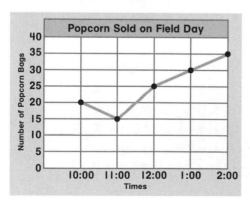

liter (page 417)

Used to measure how much larger containers hold.

median (page 279)

The **median** of 1, 3, 4, 5, and 7 is 4.

1, 3, 4, 5, 7
        ↑_____ **median**

meter (page 415)

Used to measure distances and the length of longer objects.

milliliter (page 417)

Used to measure how much small containers hold.

minute (page 243)

missing addend (page 89)

$9 + ? = 15$

↑
missing addend

mode (page 279)

The number that appears most often.

1, 3, 4, 4, 6, 7

4 is the mode.

month (page 261)

January						
Sunday	Monday	Tuesday	Wednesday	Thursday	Friday	Saturday
				1	2	3
4	5	6	7	8	9	10
11	12	13	14	15	16	17
18	19	20	21	22	23	24
25	26	27	28	29	30	31

more likely (page 299)

Green is a **more likely** outcome.

most likely (page 299)

Blue is the **most likely** outcome.

multiplication sentence
(page 527)

$4 \times 3 = 12$

$3 \times 4 = 12$

multiply (page 523)

To join equal groups.

number sentence (page 75)

$4 + 2 = 6$

$9 - 2 = 7$

$5 \times 2 = 10$

odd (page 25)

1, 3, 5, 7, 9

one dollar (page 211)

$1.00

ones (page 5)

2 ones

ordinal number (page 35)

1st   2nd   3rd
first second third

ounce (page 405)

A slice of bread weighs about 1 **ounce**.

outcome (page 293)

The possible **outcomes** are green or yellow.

parallelogram (page 317)

pattern unit (page 359)

↑
pattern unit

perimeter (page 431)

2 centimeters

2 centimeters   2 centimeters

2 centimeters

The distance around a figure. The **perimeter** measures 8 centimeters.

pictograph (page 57)

Hand We Use to Write					
right	☺	☺	☺		
left	☺	☺			

Key: Each ☺ stands for 5 children.

pint (page 401)

1 pint = 2 cups

plane shapes (page 317)

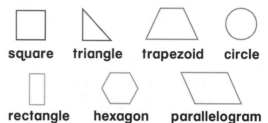

square   triangle   trapezoid   circle

rectangle   hexagon   parallelogram

point (page 281)

This grid shows **points** where events are found at Field Day.

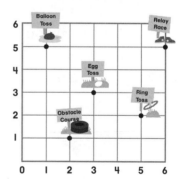

pound (page 405)

A loaf of bread weighs about 1 **pound**.

product (page 523)

$$4 \times 5 = 20$$

pyramid (page 331)

quart (page 401)

I quart = 4 cups

range (page 279)

The difference between the greatest and least number after the numbers are put in order from least to greatest.

4, 5, 6, 8, 9, 12

$$12 - 4 = 8$$

rectangle (page 317)

rectangular prism (page 331)

reflection (page 351)

A **reflection** looks like the figure flipped.

regroup (page 111 and page 147)

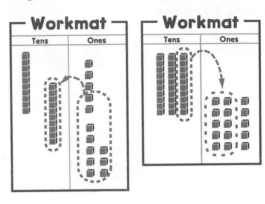

round (page 43)

To estimate to the nearest ten.

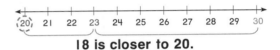

18 is closer to 20.

side (page 319)

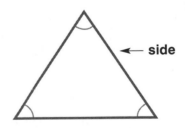

← side

skip-count (page 493)

460, 462, 464, 466, 468,...

slide (page 349)

solid figures (page 331)

sphere (page 331)

square (page 317)

square corner (page 319)

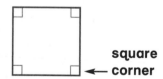

square ← corner

subtract (page 87)

To take away objects from a group or to compare groups.

sum (page 67)

$$6 + 3 = 9$$

The **sum** is 9.

survey (page 51)

The tally table shows the results of a **survey**.

Our Favorite Colors	
Color	**Tally**
blue	⊞⊞ ⅠⅠ
red	ⅠⅠⅠ
green	⊞⊞ ⊞⊞ ⅠⅠ

symmetry (page 347)

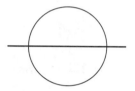

tally table (page 51)

Our Favorite Places	
Place	**Tally**
arcade	⊞⊞ ⊞⊞
park	⊞⊞
beach	⊞⊞ ⊞⊞ ⊞⊞

temperature (page 389)

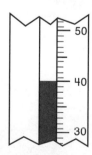

The temperature is 40°F.

tens (page 5)

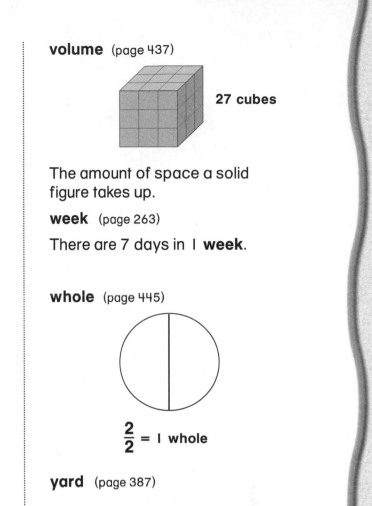

2 tens

trapezoid (page 317)

triangle (page 317)

turn (page 349)

unlikely (page 297)

Blue is an **unlikely** outcome.

volume (page 437)

27 cubes

The amount of space a solid figure takes up.

week (page 263)

There are 7 days in 1 **week**.

whole (page 445)

$\frac{2}{2}$ = 1 whole

yard (page 387)

1 **yard** = 3 feet

A baseball bat is about 1 **yard** long.

WHAT WE ARE LEARNING
Numbers to 100

VOCABULARY

Here are the vocabulary words we use in class:

Tens and **ones** The value of the digits in 2-digit numbers

For example: 28

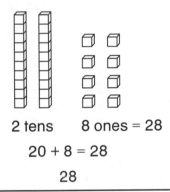

2 tens   8 ones = 28
20 + 8 = 28
28

Digits 0, 1, 2, 3, 4, 5, 6, 7, 8, and 9 are digits. In the number 42, the value of the digit 4 is 40.

Name _____

Date

Dear Family,

Your child is using place value to read and write numbers to 100. Here are some strategies your child is using to learn numbers to 100.

Grouping tens
You can group objects in tens.

For example:

1 ten is the same as 10 ones.

Writing tens and ones
You can write two-digit numbers as tens and ones.

For example:

Count to tell how many tens and ones there are.
Say: 1 ten 6 ones = 16
Or: 10 + 6 = 16

Understanding place value
You know the value of a digit based on its place in a two-digit number.

For example: in the number 43, the digit 4 has a value of 40 and the digit 3 has a value of 3.

Tens	Ones
4	3

Reading and writing numbers
You can read and write a two-digit number different ways.

For example: thirty-seven can be written as 3 tens 7 ones or 30 + 7 or 37.

Help your child use these strategies and the activity that follows to practice reading and writing numbers up to 100.

Sincerely,

Naming Tens and Ones

Your child can use small objects to model each number.

1. Write two-digit numbers on slips of paper. For example:

18	24	37
46	52	63
75	88	92

2. Place the slips in a small container, such as a paper bag.

3. Have your child pull out a slip of paper and read the number on the paper.

4. Suggest that your child use paper clips to model the number in the chart.

5. Have your child tell how many tens and ones there are for each number.

6. Have your child write the number in different ways. For example, 18 can be written as:

1 ten **8** ones,

10 + **8**,

18 .

Tens	Ones

Answers: For the example shown: 1 ten 8 ones, 10 + 8, 18; **24:** 2 tens 4 ones, 20 + 4, 24; **37:** 3 tens 7 ones, 30 + 7, 37; **46:** 4 tens 6 ones, 40 + 6, 46; **52:** 5 tens 2 ones, 50 + 2, 52; **63:** 6 tens 3 ones, 60 + 3, 63; **75:** 7 tens 5 ones, 70 + 5, 75; **88:** 8 tens 8 ones, 80 + 8, 88; **92:** 9 tens 2 ones, 90 + 2, 92

Name _____

Numbers to 100

Circle groups of tens.
Write how many tens and ones there are.
Write the number in different ways.

1. ●●●●● ●●●●●
   ●●●●● ●●●●●
   ●●●●● ●
   ●●●●● ●

   ☐ tens ☐ ones = ☐
   ☐ + ☐ = ☐
   ☐

2. ●●●●●
   ●●●●●
   ●●●●●
   ●●

   ☐ ten ☐ ones = ☐
   ☐ + ☐ = ☐
   ☐

3. ●●●●● ●●●●● ●●
   ●●●●● ●●●●● ●
   ●●●●● ●●●●●
   ●●●●● ●●●●●

   ☐ tens ☐ ones = ☐
   ☐ + ☐ = ☐
   ☐

4. ●●●●● ●●●●●
   ●●●●● ●●●
   ●●●●●
   ●●●●●

   ☐ tens ☐ ones = ☐
   ☐ + ☐ = ☐
   ☐

5. Read the tens and ones.
   Write the number.

Tens	Ones	Number
1	6	16
5	0	
6	8	
9	5	

6. Read the number. Write
   how many tens and ones.

Number	Tens	Ones
37	3	7
40		
81		
77		

Answers: 1. 3 tens 2 ones = 32, 30 + 2 = 32, 32; **2.** 1 ten 7 ones = 17, 10 + 7 = 17, 17; **3.** 4 tens 3 ones = 43, 40 + 3 = 43, 43; **4.** 2 tens 8 ones = 28, 20 + 8 = 28, 28; **5.** 50, 68, 95; **6.** 4 tens 0 ones, 8 tens 1 one, 7 tens 7 ones

Family Involvement Activities   FA3

Family Fun Cover Up

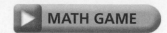

1. Cut out the squares on the right.
2. Place the squares in a small bag.
3. Take turns pulling out a square and reading the value written on the square.
4. Match the square with the number that has the same value.
5. Cover up the number by placing the square on top of it.
6. Once all numbers are covered, uncover the gameboard one square at a time, reading each value and removing the square to show the number.

83	50	75
67	29	42
91	84	73
59	66	57
38	18	27
25	80	45

7 tens 5 ones	5 tens 0 ones
6 tens 7 ones	3 tens 8 ones
4 tens 2 ones	1 ten 8 ones
9 tens 1 one	2 tens 9 ones
7 tens 3 ones	2 tens 7 ones
5 tens 9 ones	8 tens 4 ones
5 tens 7 ones	8 tens 3 ones
6 tens 6 ones	2 tens 5 ones
8 tens 0 ones	4 tens 5 ones

HARCOURT MATH
GRADE 2
Chapter 2

WHAT WE ARE LEARNING
Number Patterns

VOCABULARY

Here are the vocabulary words we use in class:

A number is **even** if it can be divided into pairs with no extras left over.

4 is even.

A number is **odd** if, when it is divided into pairs, there is one extra left over.

5 is odd.

Name _____

Date _____

Dear Family,

Your child is learning about number patterns. Here is a summary of our class discussion.

Counting forward and backward
You can use a number line to count forward or backward by ones. To count from 86 to 80, count backward: 86, 85, 84, 83, 82, 81, 80.

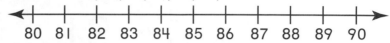

Skip counting
You can skip-count by twos (2, 4, 6, 8, 10, . . .), fives (5, 10, 15, 20, . . .), and tens (10, 20, 30, 40, . . .). You can start at any number to skip-count. For example, you can start at 35 to count by fives: 35, 40, 45, 50, ...

1	2	3	4	5	6	7	8	9	10
11	12	13	14	15	16	17	18	19	20
21	22	23	24	25	26	27	28	29	30
31	32	33	34	35	36	37	38	39	40
41	42	43	44	45	46	47	48	49	50
51	52	53	54	55	56	57	58	59	60
61	62	63	64	65	66	67	68	69	70
71	72	73	74	75	76	77	78	79	80
81	82	83	84	85	86	87	88	89	90
91	92	93	94	95	96	97	98	99	100

Even and odd
To determine if a number is even or odd, you can show the number using small objects, and then pair the objects. If no objects are left over, then the number is even. If one object is left over, then the number is odd.

Number patterns occur in all areas of mathematics, from regrouping in addition to counting the number of sides of geometric shapes. Together, enjoy the activities that follow for practice with patterns.

Sincerely,

Counting Forward and Backward

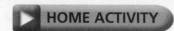

Materials yardstick or tape measure

Directions

1. Cut out the number cards. Mix them up and place them face down.

2. Take turns. Take a number card. Read the number. Count forward or backward from the number to get to 25.

You can use the yardstick or tape measure as a number line to help you count. First, locate the card's number on the yardstick or tape measure. Count the numbers going to the right or to the left until you say "25".

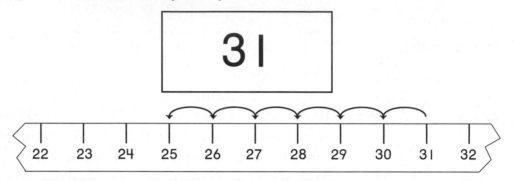

3. When you reach 25, place the card in a discard pile and let the next person take a turn.

14	15	16	17
18	19	20	21
29	30	31	32
33	34	35	36

Name_____

Number Patterns

Write the missing numbers.
Use the number line to help you.

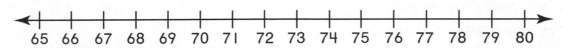

65 66 67 68 69 70 71 72 73 74 75 76 77 78 79 80

1. Count forward to 76.

70, _____, _____, _____, _____, _____, _____

2. Count backward to 74.

80, _____, _____, _____, _____, _____, _____

3. Count backward to 67.

73, _____, _____, _____, _____, _____, _____

Count by fives.

4. 0, 5, 10, _____, _____, _____, _____, _____

5. 35, 40, 45, _____, _____, _____, _____, _____

Draw the number of cubes.
Write *even* or *odd*.

6. 25	7. 16
_____	_____

Answers: 1. 71, 72, 73, 74, 75, 76; **2.** 79, 78, 77, 76, 75, 74; **3.** 72, 71, 70, 69, 68, 67; **4.** 15, 20, 25, 30, 35; **5.** 50, 55, 60, 65, 70; **6.** odd; **7.** even

Family Involvement Activities   FA7

Family Fun   Evens and Odds
2 4   1 3

Game for 2 players

Materials   20 small objects, such as paper clips or pennies

1. Decide which of you will get points for even numbers, and which of you will get points for odd numbers.

2. Write your names in a table below.

3. On the count of three, each of you holds up from 1 through 10 fingers.

4. Count all of the fingers. If the number is even, the even player gets one point. If the number is odd, the odd player gets one point. If you are not sure whether the number is even or odd, pair up small objects to see.

5. Use the table to tally your points. The first player to get five points wins the game.

Game 1	
Players	**Points**
Even _____	
Odd _____	

Game 2	
Players	**Points**
Even _____	
Odd _____	

Game 3	
Players	**Points**
Even _____	
Odd _____	

Game 4	
Players	**Points**
Even _____	
Odd _____	

Game 5	
Players	**Points**
Even _____	
Odd _____	

Game 6	
Players	**Points**
Even _____	
Odd _____	

HARCOURT MATH

GRADE 2

Chapter 3

WHAT WE ARE LEARNING

Comparing and Ordering
Numbers

VOCABULARY

Here are the vocabulary
words we use in class:

Ordinal number A
number that names a
position.
ABCDEFG
C is the third (3rd) letter.

Is greater than > Use
this symbol to compare two
numbers.

$$27 > 19$$

27 is greater than 19.

Is less than < Use this
symbol to compare two
numbers.

$$19 < 27$$

19 is less than 27.

Use this equal to =
symbol to show that two
amounts are the same.

$$12 = 12$$

12 is equal to 12.

Name _____

Date

Dear Family,

Your child is using ordinal numbers to describe an
object's position and learning to compare numbers
using the words and symbols for *greater than, less than,*
and *equal to.*

This is how your child compares 35 and 17.

• **STEP 1** Model the numbers.

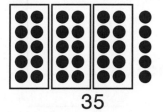 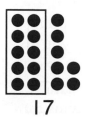

35   17

• **STEP 2** Compare the tens. 3 tens is more than 1 ten.

• **STEP 3** Compare the numbers.

35 is *greater than* 17 because 3 tens is more than 1 ten.

$$35 > 17$$

or   17 is *less than* 35 because 1 ten is less than 3 tens.

$$17 < 35$$

Your child is describing number order using the words
before, after, and *between.*

43 is just **before** 44.   45 is just **after** 44.

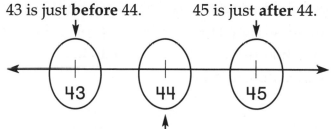

44 is **between** 43 and 45.

Use the activities that follow to practice comparing and
ordering numbers.

Sincerely,

Comparing Numbers

1. Cut out the numbers on page FA13.
2. Put the numbers in a container, such as a shoe box.
3. Have your child select two numbers.
4. Have your child place the numbers in the squares on the right to show which number is greater than (>) the other. Then have him or her show which number is less than (<) the other.
5. Have your child use objects to model the numbers as needed.

greater than

less than

Ordering Numbers

1. Have your child select one number from the shoe box and place the number in the square below.
2. Have your child name the number that comes just before his or her number.
3. Have your child name the number that comes just after his or her number.
4. Have your child use the word *between* to tell more about his or her number.
5. Repeat with a new number.

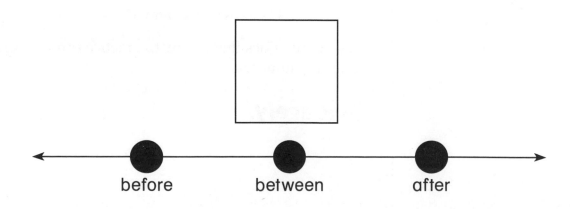

before   between   after

Name_____

Comparing and Ordering Numbers

Write the ordinal number that is just after.

1. 67th _____   2. 42nd _____   3. 18th _____

Write greater than, less than, or equal to.
Then write >, <, or =.

4. 25 is _____ 22.   5. 33 is _____ 38.

    25 ◯ 22   33 ◯ 38

6. 63 is _____ 65.   7. 54 is _____ 54.

    63 ◯ 65   54 ◯ 54

Write the missing number.

8. ←•———•———•→   9. ←•———•———•→

   65 ___ 67   ___ 46   47

Write the missing numbers.

10. 85, 75, 65, ____, 45, ____, ____, ____

11. 27, ____, 47, 57, ____, 77, ____, ____

Answers: 1. 68th; 2. 43rd; 3. 19th; 4. greater than, >; 5. less than, <; 6. less than, <; 7. equal to, =; 8. 66; 9. 45; 10. 55, 35, 25, 15; 11. 37, 67, 87, 97

Family Involvement Activities   FA11

Family Fun Laundry Line

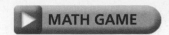

1. Cut out each shirt box at the bottom of the page.

2. Use string or ribbon to make the clothesline on the page longer.

3. Take turns selecting a shirt and hanging it on the clothesline. Shirts should be hung in order from least to greatest.

4. Use the words *before*, *after*, or *between* to tell about the number.
   Note: You may have to move a shirt in order to add a new shirt to the clothesline.

5. Continue until all the shirts are hung up to dry.

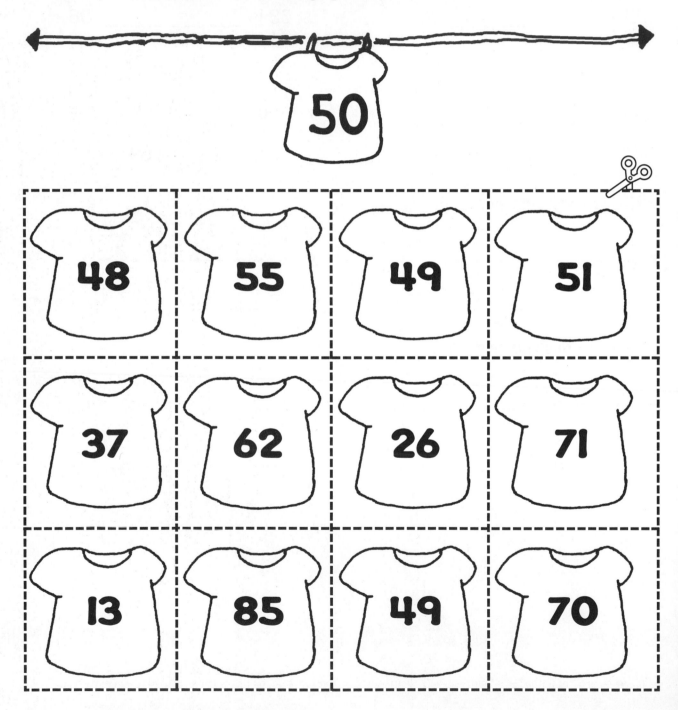

Cut out the number boxes.
Use with page FA10.

58	91	27	72	25	53
2	4	6	8	10	12
13	15	17	19	21	23
30	31	33	35	37	39
42	44	46	48	50	52
60	62	64	66	68	70
73	75	77	79	80	81
85	87	90	92	94	96

WHAT WE ARE LEARNING

Tables and Graphs

VOCABULARY

Here are the vocabulary words we use in class:

Pictograph A graph that uses pictures to stand for numbers

OUR PETS				
Cats	🐱	🐱	🐱	🐱
Dogs	🐶	🐶	🐶	
Birds	🐦			

Bar graph A graph that uses bars to stand for numbers

OUR PETS				
Cats	▓	▓	▓	▓
Dogs	▓	▓	▓	
Birds	▓			
	0 1 2 3 4			

Name _____

Date

Dear Family,

Your child is learning how to gather data by taking a survey, how to organize data in tally tables and in graphs, and how to use the tables and graphs to answer questions and to make predictions.

Your child uses tally tables to record survey results. This tally table shows that there are 5 birthdays in the fall.

CHILDREN'S BIRTHDAY SEASONS	
Season	Tally
winter	|||
spring	||
summer	||||
fall	|||||

Your child can use either real objects or data from a tally table to make a graph. Your child might line up different types of fruit to make a **concrete graph**.

Your child might use data in a tally table to make a picture graph or a bar graph.

Use the activities that follow to help your child make graphs and answer questions about graphs.

Sincerely,

Bunches of Balls

Make a bar graph to show how many of each type of ball there are.

		Number of Balls			
6					
5					
4					
3					
2					
1					
0	Beach Balls	Footballs	Tennis Balls	Baseballs	Basketballs

Use the bar graph to answer the questions.

1. How many beach balls are there? ☐

2. How many tennis balls and baseballs are there in all? ☐

3. How many more tennis balls than basketballs are there? ☐

Answers: The bar graph will have the following squares shaded: 4 in the beach ball column, 2 in the football column, 6 in the tennis ball column, 3 in the baseball column, and 1 in the basketball column.
1. 4; 2. 9; 3. 5 more

Name _____

Tables and Graphs

Use the tally tables to answer the questions.

NEXT DOOR NEIGHBORS' FAVORITE JAMS	
apricot	|||
cherry		
grape		
strawberry	||

NEIGHBORHOOD'S FAVORITE JAMS	
apricot	||||| ||||| |||
cherry	|||||
grape	||||| ||
strawberry	||||| |||||	

1. Which jam was chosen most often by the next door neighbors? _____

2. Which jam was chosen least often by people in the neighborhood? _____

Use the tally table to fill in the picture graph.
Draw 😊 for every 5 children.

3.

CHILDREN'S FAVORITE FLOWERS	
Flower	Tally
rose	||||| ||||| |||||
tulip	||||| |||||
daisy	||||| ||||| ||||| |||||

CHILDREN'S FAVORITE FLOWERS					
rose					
tulip					
daisy					

Key: Each 😊 stands for 5 children

Use the pictograph to answer the questions.

4. Which flower got 10 votes? _____

5. Which flower got the most votes? _____

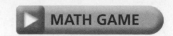

Family Fun
Find the Animals

1. Find the animals hidden in the picture.
2. Complete the bar graph to show how many of each animal there are.
   Hint: You might want to color each type of animal a different color.

Number of Animals

5				
4				
3				
2				
1				
0				

Answers: The bar graph will have the following squares shaded: 2 in the dog column, 5 in the fish column, 3 in the kitten column, 1 in the turtle column

HARCOURT MATH
GRADE 2
Chapter 5

WHAT WE ARE LEARNING

Addition Strategies

VOCABULARY

Here are the vocabulary words we use in class:

Count on To add by counting forward from the greater number

Sum The answer when numbers are added

Doubles
  6 + 6 = 12

Doubles plus one
Addition facts whose sums are one more than the sum of a doubles fact

doubles
  6 + 6 = 12

doubles plus one
  6 + 7 = 13

Addend any of the numbers that are added

Add To join two groups

Number sentence A sentence that includes numbers, operation symbols, and greater than or less than symbol or an equal sign.

Name _____

Date

Dear Family,

Your child is using addition strategies to learn facts to 20. These are the strategies your child is using:

Order property

You can add numbers in any order, and the sum will be the same.

$$\begin{array}{r} 5 \\ + 3 \\ \hline 8 \end{array} \qquad \begin{array}{r} 3 \\ + 5 \\ \hline 8 \end{array}$$

For example: 5 + 3 and 3 + 5 both equal 8.

Zero property

When you add zero to a number, the sum is the number you started with.

$$\begin{array}{r} 12 \\ + 0 \\ \hline 12 \end{array}$$

For example: 12 + 0 equals 12.

Count on 1, 2, or 3

When adding 1, 2, or 3, you can count on from the greater number to find the sum.

$$\begin{array}{r} 6 \\ + 3 \\ \hline 9 \end{array}$$

Start with the larger number, which is 6.
Count on 3: 7, 8, 9
The sum is 9.

Doubles and doubles plus one

You can use doubles facts to help you learn doubles-plus-one facts.

4 + 4 = 8   This is a doubles fact.

4 + 5 = 9   This is a doubles-plus-one fact.
         4 + 4 is 8; 8 + 1 is 9.

continued on page FA20

Work Together

Find the sums.
Use the strategies.

1. $4 + 7 =$ ___
2. $7 + 4 =$ ___

3. $17 + 0 =$ ___
4. $0 + 17 =$ ___

5. $8 + 3 =$ ___
6. $7 + 2 =$ ___
7. $12 + 1 =$ ___

8. $5 + 5 =$ ___
9. $5 + 6 =$ ___
10. $5 + 4 =$ ___

11. $8 + 5 =$ ___

12. $3 + 7 + 8 =$ ___
13. $5 + 4 + 6 =$ ___
14. $4 + 2 + 4 =$ ___
15. $8 + 8 + 4 =$ ___
16. $9 + 2 + 9 =$ ___

More addition strategies:
Make a ten

You can find sums by making a ten. You can use counters to help.

$$\begin{array}{r} 9 \\ + \ 4 \\ \hline 13 \end{array}$$

Count out 9 pennies; count out 4 pennies; move 1 penny from the group of 4 to the group of 9 to make a ten.

Think:

$$\begin{array}{r} 10 \\ + \ 3 \\ \hline 13 \end{array}$$

$10 + 3 = 13$
So, $9 + 4 = 13$

Add three numbers

Add two numbers. Then add the third number to the sum. Use addition strategies to help you add.

$2 + 6 + 8 = 16$

1. Choose 2 numbers to add: $2 + 8 = 10$
2. Add the second number to find the sum: $10 + 6 = 16$
3. So, $2 + 6 + 8 = 16$

OR

1. Choose 2 different numbers to add: $2 + 6 = 8$
2. Add the third number to find the sum: $8 + 8 = 16$
3. So, $2 + 6 + 8 = 16$

Help your child use these addition strategies and the exercises on the left of the page to practice sums to 20.

Sincerely,

Addition Strategies

Write the sums. You may wish to use pennies
or other objects to model each problem.

1. $3 + 6 =$ ☐

2. $5 + 8 =$ ☐

3. $8 + 0 =$ ☐

4. $6 + 3 =$ ☐

5. $4 + 6 =$ ☐

6. $0 + 12 =$ ☐

7. $9 + 2 =$ ☐

8. $12 + 1 =$ ☐

9. $3 + 3 =$ ☐

Write the sums.

10. $6 + 6 =$ ☐

$6 + 7 =$ ☐

11. $5 + 5 =$ ☐

$5 + 6 =$ ☐

12. $7 + 7 =$ ☐

$7 + 8 =$ ☐

Circle two numbers to add first. Then solve.

13. $1 + 5 + 9 =$ ☐

14. $8 + 0 + 4 =$ ☐

15. $3 + 5 + 7 =$ ☐

16. $2 + 6 + 2 =$ ☐

17. $3 + 2 + 5 =$ ☐

18. $4 + 6 + 5 =$ ☐

19. Draw circles to show $5 + 9$.

Write the number sentence.

___ ◯ ___ ◯ ___

Family Fun Color the Sum

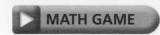

1. Cut out the addition facts.
2. Place the slips of paper in a container, such as a small box or bag.
3. Take turns. Select a slip of paper; find the sum, and color the square that shows the sum. (Each player uses a different color.)
4. Continue until all squares have been colored.
5. The player with the most squares colored is the winner.

5 + 0	3 + 3	8 + 3 + 2
3 + 4	4 + 4	2 + 6 + 8
3 + 7	7 + 3	6 + 7 + 4
9 + 2	8 + 4	4 + 8 + 2
7 + 7	8 + 7	9 + 1 + 5
9 + 9	3 + 5	8 + 2 + 7
8 + 1	4 + 6	8 + 8 + 2
3 + 8	4 + 8	6 + 4 + 4
7 + 6	7 + 9	3 + 5 + 7

5	6	7	8	9
10	11	12	13	14
15	16	17	18	8
9	10	11	12	13
14	15	16	17	18

WHAT WE ARE LEARNING

Subtraction Strategies

VOCABULARY

Here are the vocabulary words we use in class:

Count back To subtract by counting backward from the greater number

Difference The answer to a subtraction problem

Fact family A group of addition and subtraction facts that use the same numbers

For example, here is the fact family for the numbers 5, 6, and 11.

$$5 + 6 = 11$$
$$6 + 5 = 11$$
$$11 - 5 = 6$$
$$11 - 6 = 5$$

Subtract To find how many are left when a number of items are taken away from a group of items; to find the difference when two groups are compared

Missing Addend

Sometimes an addend is missing.

$$3 + ? = 7$$

addend   addend

Name _____

Date

Dear Family,

Your child is learning to subtract from numbers through 20. These are the subtraction strategies your child is using:

Subtract all or zero

$$\begin{array}{r} 8 \\ -8 \\ \hline 0 \end{array}$$

When you subtract all from a number, you have zero left.

$$\begin{array}{r} 8 \\ -0 \\ \hline 8 \end{array}$$

When you subtract zero from a number, you have the same number you started with.

Count back

When you subtract 1, 2, or 3, you can count back to find how many are left.

$$\begin{array}{r} 10 \\ -2 \\ \hline 8 \end{array}$$

For example, to find the difference for $10 - 2$, say: 10; count back two: 9, 8. So, $10 - 2 = 8$.

Think addition to subtract

You can use an addition fact you know to help you find the difference.

$$\begin{array}{r} 15 \\ -6 \\ \hline ? \end{array} \qquad \begin{array}{r} 9 \\ +6 \\ \hline 15 \end{array}$$

If you know $9 + 6 = 15$, then you know $15 - 6 = 9$.

Fact families

When you know an addition fact, you can use the same numbers to write the fact family.

$$\begin{array}{r} 7 \\ +6 \\ \hline 13 \end{array} \qquad \begin{array}{r} 13 \\ -6 \\ \hline 7 \end{array} \qquad \begin{array}{r} 6 \\ +7 \\ \hline 13 \end{array} \qquad \begin{array}{r} 13 \\ -7 \\ \hline 6 \end{array}$$

Help your child use these strategies and the activities that follow to practice subtracting.

Sincerely,

Finding Differences

1. Cut out the subtraction facts below.
2. Have your child select a fact.
3. Have your child find the difference.
4. For each fact, ask how your child found the difference.

5. To check, suggest that your child model the fact using small objects such as paper clips or pennies.

Tip: If your child has difficulty with a problem, work together to solve it. Then randomly place the card in the pile of unsolved problems so your child will have an opportunity to solve the problem again.

Sample Problems

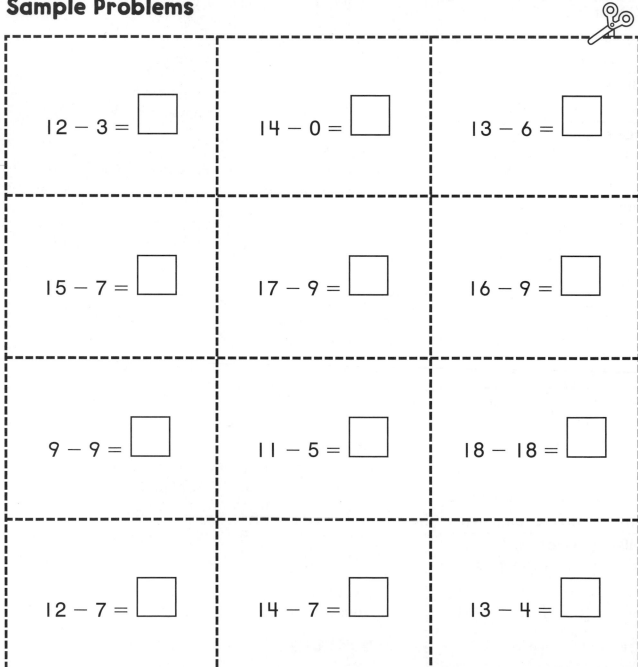

12 − 3 = ☐	14 − 0 = ☐	13 − 6 = ☐
15 − 7 = ☐	17 − 9 = ☐	16 − 9 = ☐
9 − 9 = ☐	11 − 5 = ☐	18 − 18 = ☐
12 − 7 = ☐	14 − 7 = ☐	13 − 4 = ☐

Name_____

Subtraction Strategies

Solve.
You may wish to use objects to model each problem.

1. $8 - 0 = \boxed{}$ 2. $16 - 16 = \boxed{}$ 3. $11 - 0 = \boxed{}$

4. $9 - 3 = \boxed{}$ 5. $14 - 6 = \boxed{}$ 6. $17 - 17 = \boxed{}$

7. $11 - 9 = \boxed{}$ 8. $12 - 7 = \boxed{}$ 9. $15 - 6 = \boxed{}$

Complete each fact family.

10. $4 + 8 = \boxed{}$ 11. $5 + 10 = \boxed{}$ 12. $7 + 3 = \boxed{}$

$8 + \boxed{} = \boxed{}$ $\boxed{} + 5 = \boxed{}$ $3 + \boxed{} = \boxed{}$

$\boxed{} - 8 = \boxed{}$ $\boxed{} - 5 = \boxed{}$ $\boxed{} - 7 = \boxed{}$

$\boxed{} - 4 = \boxed{}$ $\boxed{} - 10 = \boxed{}$ $\boxed{} - 3 = \boxed{}$

Use the numbers in each box to write a fact family.

| 7, 9, 16 | 5, 8, 13 |

13. $\boxed{} + \boxed{} = \boxed{}$ 14. $\boxed{} + \boxed{} = \boxed{}$

$\boxed{} + \boxed{} = \boxed{}$ $\boxed{} + \boxed{} = \boxed{}$

$\boxed{} - \boxed{} = \boxed{}$ $\boxed{} - \boxed{} = \boxed{}$

$\boxed{} - \boxed{} = \boxed{}$ $\boxed{} - \boxed{} = \boxed{}$

Answers: 1. 8; **2.** 0; **3.** 11; **4.** 6; **5.** 8; **6.** 0; **7.** 2; **8.** 5; **9.** 9; **10.** 4 + 8 = 12, 8 + 4 = 12, 12 − 8 = 4, 12 − 4 = 8;
11. 5 + 10 = 15, 10 + 5 = 15, 15 − 5 = 10, 15 − 10 = 5; **12.** 7 + 3 = 10, 3 + 7 = 10, 10 − 7 = 3, 10 − 3 = 7;
13. 7 + 9 = 16, 9 + 7 = 16, 16 − 7 = 9, 16 − 9 = 7; **14.** 5 + 8 = 13, 8 + 5 = 13, 13 − 5 = 8, 13 − 8 = 5

Family Fun
Fishing for Facts

1. Cut apart the fish cards on the dotted lines. Place them face down in rows of 3.
2. The first player chooses two cards and finds the difference for each fact. If the differences are the same, the player keeps the cards and takes another turn. If the differences are not the same, the cards are replaced in their original positions, and the next player takes a turn.
3. Play continues until all matches have been made. The player with more cards at the end of the game is the winner.

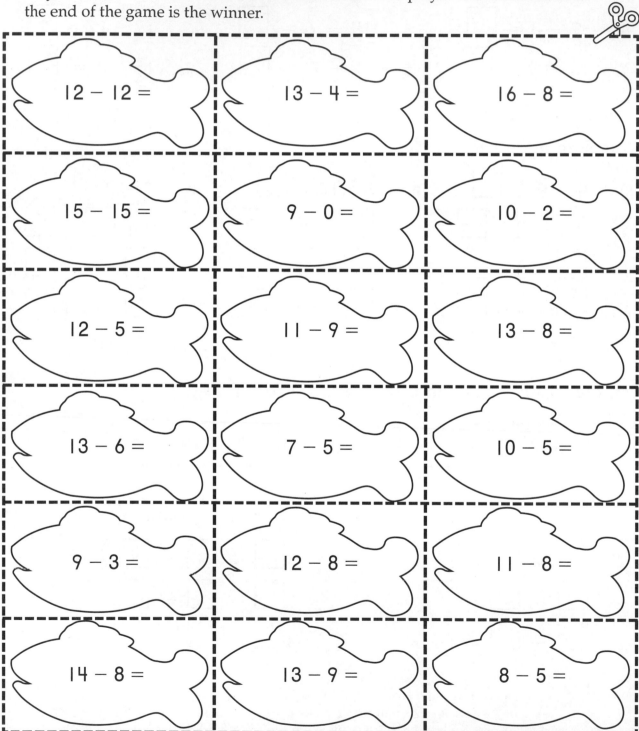

12 − 12 =	13 − 4 =	16 − 8 =
15 − 15 =	9 − 0 =	10 − 2 =
12 − 5 =	11 − 9 =	13 − 8 =
13 − 6 =	7 − 5 =	10 − 5 =
9 − 3 =	12 − 8 =	11 − 8 =
14 − 8 =	13 − 9 =	8 − 5 =

HARCOURT MATH
GRADE 2
Chapter 7

WHAT WE ARE LEARNING

Explore 2-Digit Addition

VOCABULARY

Here is a vocabulary word that we use in class:

Regroup When you add 2-digit numbers, sometimes you need to **regroup.**

For example:

38 + 4

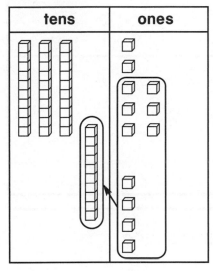

Regroup 10 ones as 1 ten.

Name

Date

Dear Family,

Your child is learning concepts of 2-digit addition. Here are some ways your child is learning to add.

Use an addition fact

$$\begin{array}{rr} 50 & 5 \text{ tens} \\ +30 & +3 \text{ tens} \\ \hline 80 & 8 \text{ tens} \end{array}$$

Count on tens or ones

You can count on by ones or by tens.

$34 + 3 = 37$
Say the greater number: 34.
Count on 3 ones from 34: 35, 36, 37.
$34 + 3 = 37$

$65 + 20 = 85$
Say the greater number: 65.
Count on 20, which is two tens: 75, 85.
$65 + 20 = 85$

Use tens and ones blocks

Show $24 + 8$ with blocks. If there are 10 or more ones, regroup.

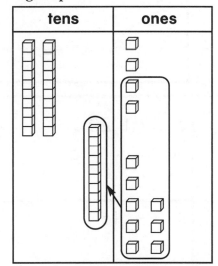

So, when you add $24 + 8$, you end up with 3 tens and 2 ones.

Help your child use the activity that follows to practice adding 2-digit numbers.

Sincerely,

Adding 1-Digit and 2-Digit Numbers

1. Gather small objects, such as toothpicks or straws (cut straws in half).

2. Help your child bundle the objects in groups of 10.

3. Have your child choose whether to find the sum by using an addition fact, by counting on, or by using the objects and the work area to the right.

4. Have your child read each addition problem and talk about how he or she solved the problem.

tens	ones
+	

1. $35 + 2$	2. $50 + 20$	3. $16 + 9$
4. $13 + 28$	5. $3 + 46$	6. $27 + 15$
7. $23 + 16$	8. $30 + 20$	9. $52 + 1$

FA28   Family Involvement Activities

Name _____

Explore 2-Digit Addition

Count on to add.

1. $45 + 3 = \boxed{48}$ $26 + 2 = \square$ $64 + 1 = \square$

2. $30 + 54 = \square$ $42 + 20 = \square$ $67 + 10 = \square$

Use objects to show each problem. Add.
Circle the problems that needed regrouping.

tens	ones

3. $18 + 6$

_____ tens _____ ones

4. $24 + 4$

_____ tens _____ ones

5. $23 + 15$

_____ tens _____ ones

6. $36 + 14$

_____ tens _____ ones

7. $23 + 12$

_____ tens _____ ones

Answers: 1. 48, 28, 65; **2.** 84, 62, 77; **3.** 2 tens 4 ones (circled); **4.** 2 tens 8 ones; **5.** 3 tens 8 ones; **6.** 5 tens 0 ones (circled); **7.** 3 tens 5 ones

Family Fun Hidden Picture

1. Have your child write a number between 10 and 50 on a piece of paper.

2. Choose another number between 1 and 19, and have your child write this number next to the first one.

3. Ask your child to add the two numbers. Have him or her use small objects or draw a picture to show each problem.

4. Check your child's work.

5. Ask your child if regrouping was used to solve the problem.
   If YES, have your child color one puzzle piece with an "R" on it green.
   If NO, have your child color one blank puzzle piece brown.

6. Repeat steps 1 to 6 until your child has colored all the puzzle pieces marked with an "R."

7. When all the pieces with "R" are colored, a picture should be visible. What picture was hidden in the puzzle?

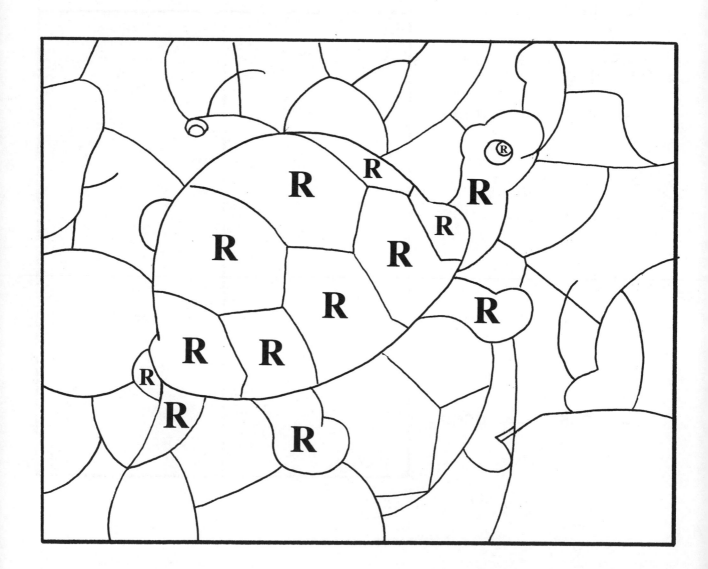

Answers: The hidden picture is a turtle.

VOCABULARY

Here is a vocabulary word that we use in class:

Regroup You regroup when you trade ten ones for one ten. For example, you can regroup fourteen ones as one ten and four ones.

Name _____

Date _____

Dear Family,

Your child is adding 1-digit and 2-digit numbers, as well as 2-digit and 2-digit numbers. Your child is rewriting horizontal addition sentences in vertical form. Examples of problems your child is doing in class follow:

Add 1-digit and 2-digit numbers

tens	ones
①	
5	8
+	7
6	5

Add the ones: $8 + 7 = 15$
Regroup 15 to make 1 ten and 5 ones.
Write 5 to show how many ones there are.
Write 1 to show the new ten. Add the tens.
Write 6 to show how many tens there are.

Add two 2-digit numbers

tens	ones
①	
3	4
+1	8
5	2

Add the ones: $4 + 8 = 12$
Regroup 12 to make 1 ten and 2 ones.
Write 2 to show how many ones there are.
Write 1 to show the new ten. Add the tens.
Write 5 to show how many tens there are.

Rewrite 2-digit addition

$45 + 18 =$ _____

tens	ones
①	
4	5
+1	8
6	3

Write 4 in the tens column.
Write 5 in the ones column.
Write 1 in the tens column.
Write 8 in the ones column.
Add. Be sure to regroup when you have 10 or more ones.

Help your child use the activity that follows to practice 2-digit addition.

Sincerely,

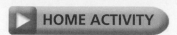
Solve 2-Digit Addition Problems

My Work Area

1. Cut out the numbers at the bottom of the page.
2. Place them in a small paper bag.
3. Have your child select two numbers and place them in any of the shaded boxes in the work area to the right.
4. Then it is your turn to select two numbers. Place them in the remaining shaded boxes.
5. Have your child write the addition problem on a separate sheet of paper.
6. Have your child solve the problem. Have him or her circle the problem if he or she regrouped.
7. Place the numbers back in the bag and repeat the activity to create a new addition problem.

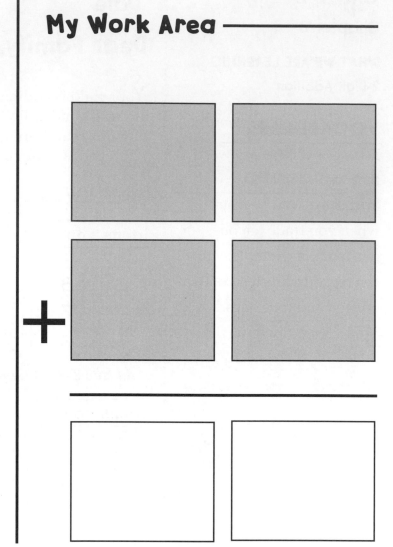

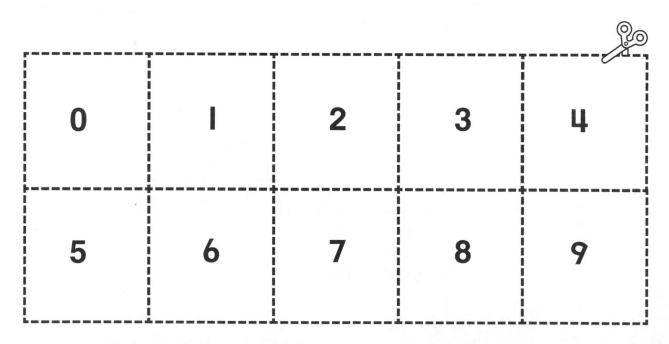

2-Digit Addition

Add. Regroup when you have 10 or more ones.

1.

tens	ones
□	
1	8
+ 3	6

tens	ones
□	
4	5
+ 2	7

tens	ones
□	
3	4
+ 1	5

2.

tens	ones
□	
2	9
+ 1	3

tens	ones
□	
4	6
+ 1	2

tens	ones
□	
4	8
+ 3	7

Rewrite the problem. Then add.

3. $35 + 17 =$ $52 + 29 =$ $63 + 36 =$

tens	ones
□	
+	

tens	ones
□	
+	

tens	ones
□	
+	

Family Fun   A Walk in the Park

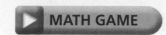

1. You will need: paper, pencils, and small objects, such as pennies or paper clips, to use as game markers.
2. On small slips of paper, write 2-digit addition problems like the sample problems on the bottom of this page.
3. Take turns selecting a slip of paper and solving the problem.
4. Work together to check each player's addition. A player moves his or her game marker forward one space for each correct answer.
5. Continue playing until all players reach the **Finish**.

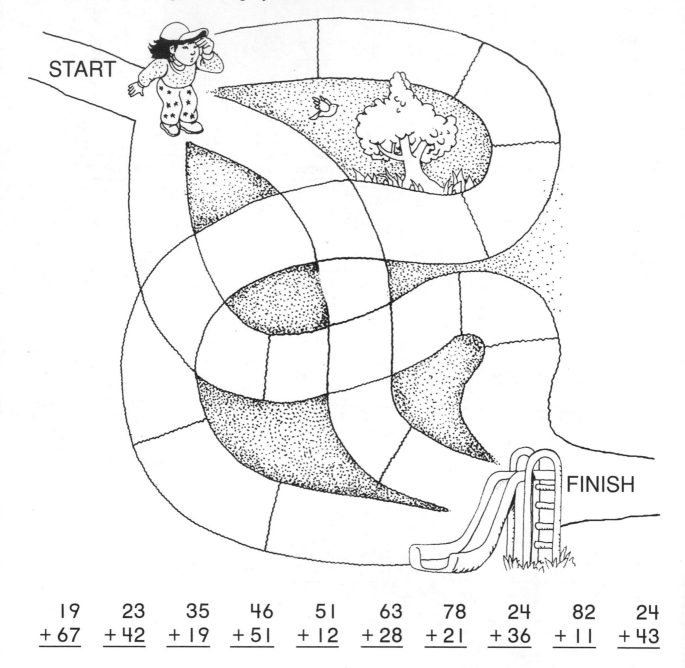

19	23	35	46	51	63	78	24	82	24
+ 67	+ 42	+ 19	+ 51	+ 12	+ 28	+ 21	+ 36	+ 11	+ 43

Answers: 19 + 67 = 86, 23 + 42 = 65, 35 + 19 = 54, 46 + 51 = 97, 51 + 12 = 63, 63 + 28 = 91, 78 + 21 = 99, 24 + 36 = 60, 82 + 11 = 93, 24 + 43 = 67

WHAT WE ARE LEARNING

Explore 2-Digit Subtraction

VOCABULARY

Here is a vocabulary word that we use in class.

Regroup When you subtract two numbers, you need to regroup when there are not enough ones to subtract from.

Sample:

tens	ones
[4]	[12]
5̶	2
− 3	4̶
1	8

Name _____

Date _____

Dear Family,

Your child is learning to subtract 2-digit numbers. Here are examples of problems your child is learning.

Subtract tens

$$50 \quad \text{Think of a fact.}$$
$$- 30 \quad 5 - 3 = 2$$
$$\overline{20} \quad 5 \text{ tens} - 3 \text{ tens} = 2 \text{ tens}$$

So, $50 - 30 = 20$

Count back ones or tens

$34 - 3 = \square$

Say the greater number: 34.

Count back 3 ones from 34: 33, 32, 31.

So, $34 - 3 = 31$.

$65 - 20 = \square$

Say the greater number: 65.

Count back 20, which is two tens: 55, 45.

So, $65 - 20 = 45$.

Model subtraction

With regrouping

tens	ones
[1]	[13]
2̶	3̶
−	5
1	8

No regrouping

tens	ones
2	9
− 1	5
1	4

With your child, do the activity that follows to practice 2-digit subtraction.

Sincerely,

Modeling Subtraction

1. Gather small objects, such as toothpicks or straws (cut straws in half).

2. Help your child rubber-band the objects into bundles of 10.

3. Have your child use the objects and the work area to the right to show the subtraction problems on this page.

4. Have your child read each subtraction problem and say the difference.

tens	ones

Find the difference.

```
  52        35        24
- 40      -  2      - 15
```

```
  42        37        34
-  5      - 15      - 18
```

```
  23        44        56
- 17      - 13      - 25
```

$60 - 30 = \boxed{}$

$56 - 3 = \boxed{}$

$47 - 30 = \boxed{}$

$30 - 10 = \boxed{}$

$29 - 3 = \boxed{}$

Explore 2-Digit Subtraction

Subtract tens.

1. $40 - 10 =$ ☐   2. $30 - 20 =$ ☐   3. $60 - 30 =$ ☐

Count back by tens or ones.

4. $38 - 2 =$ ☐   5. $42 - 20 =$ ☐   6. $67 - 10 =$ ☐

7. $49 - 3 =$ ☐   8. $56 - 2 =$ ☐   9. $75 - 30 =$ ☐

Subtract. Use objects to show each problem.
Circle the problems that needed regrouping.

10.
$$\begin{array}{r} 26 \\ -\ 2 \\ \hline \end{array}$$

11.
$$\begin{array}{r} 15 \\ -\ 5 \\ \hline \end{array}$$

12.
$$\begin{array}{r} 43 \\ -\ 8 \\ \hline \end{array}$$

13.
$$\begin{array}{r} 32 \\ -16 \\ \hline \end{array}$$

14.
$$\begin{array}{r} 23 \\ -15 \\ \hline \end{array}$$

15.
$$\begin{array}{r} 16 \\ -14 \\ \hline \end{array}$$

16.
$$\begin{array}{r} 58 \\ -41 \\ \hline \end{array}$$

17.
$$\begin{array}{r} 63 \\ -26 \\ \hline \end{array}$$

18.
$$\begin{array}{r} 37 \\ -12 \\ \hline \end{array}$$

19.
$$\begin{array}{r} 45 \\ -22 \\ \hline \end{array}$$

20.
$$\begin{array}{r} 18 \\ -15 \\ \hline \end{array}$$

21.
$$\begin{array}{r} 27 \\ -\ 8 \\ \hline \end{array}$$

Answers: 1. 30; 2. 10; 3. 30; 4. 36; 5. 22; 6. 57; 7. 46; 8. 54; 9. 45; 10. 24; 11. 10; 12. 35; 13. 16; 14. 8; 15. 2; 16. 17; 17. 37; 18. 25; 19. 23; 20. 3; 21. 19; Exercises 12, 13, 14, 17, and 21 are circled.

Family Fun Subtract and Score

Home	3
Visitors	1

 ▶ MATH GAME

1. Take turns solving the subtraction problems at the bottom of the page.

2. Ask: *Did we need to regroup to solve the problem?*
If yes: have your child make a tally mark in the box under *Regrouping.*
If no: have your child make a tally mark in the box under *No Regrouping.*

3. Continue until all problems have been solved.

4. Count the tally marks. Did you solve more problems with regrouping or without regrouping?

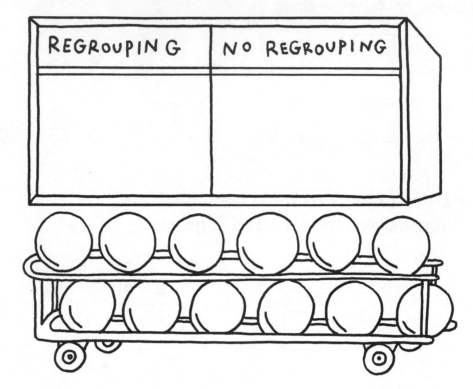

REGROUPING NO REGROUPING

1. 25 − 19	**2.** 50 − 20	**3.** 22 − 8	**4.** 36 − 3	**5.** 43 − 15	**6.** 31 − 18
7. 39 − 19	**8.** 42 − 17	**9.** 35 − 7	**10.** 26 − 2	**11.** 40 − 20	**12.** 57 − 12

Want to do more? Write more subtraction problems. Continue to tally to show when regrouping was needed and when regrouping was not needed.

Answers: 1. 6; **2.** 30; **3.** 14; **4.** 33; **5.** 28; **6.** 13; **7.** 20; **8.** 25; **9.** 28; **10.** 24; **11.** 20; **12.** 45; There should be 6 tally marks in the *Regrouping* column and 6 tally marks in the *No Regrouping* column.

FA38   Family Involvement Activities

VOCABULARY

Here are the vocabulary words we use in class:

Regroup When you subtract 2-digit numbers, sometimes you need to regroup. You can regroup 1 ten as **10 ones**

Estimate To find about how many

$30 - 10 = 20$,

so $28 - 9$ is about 20.

Name _____

Date

Dear Family,

Your child is finding more ways to subtract 2-digit numbers. He or she is also rewriting horizontal subtraction sentences in vertical form. Examples of problems your child is doing in class follow:

Subtract 2-digit numbers

tens	ones
4	18
5	8
1	9
3	9

Regroup 1 ten to make 10 ones.
Write 18 to show how many ones there are in all.
Write 4 to show how many tens there are now.
Subtract the ones. Subtract the tens.

Rewrite 2-digit subtraction

$$45 - 28 = \underline{\quad}$$

tens	ones
3	15
4	5
2	8
1	7

Write 4 in the tens column.
Write 5 in the ones column.
Write 2 in the tens column.
Write 8 in the ones column.
Subtract. Be sure to regroup when you do not have enough ones.

Estimate differences

Estimate $39 - 22$ as $40 - 20$.

$40 - 20 = 20$, so $39 - 22$ is about 20.

Help your child use the activity that follows to practice 2-digit subtraction.

Sincerely,

Solve 2-Digit Subtraction Problems

My Work Area

1. Cut out the numbers at the bottom of the page and place them in a small bag.
2. Have your child select two numbers and place them in any of the shaded boxes in the work area to the right.
3. Then it is your turn to select two numbers and place them in the remaining shaded boxes. Rearrange the numbers as needed to make a subtraction problem.
   Tip: Be sure the greater number is placed at the top.
4. Have your child write the subtraction problem on a separate sheet of paper.
5. Ask your child to solve the problem. He or she may want to use small objects to show the problem.
6. Have your child circle the problem if regrouping was needed.
7. Place the numbers back in the bag and repeat the activity to make a new subtraction problem.

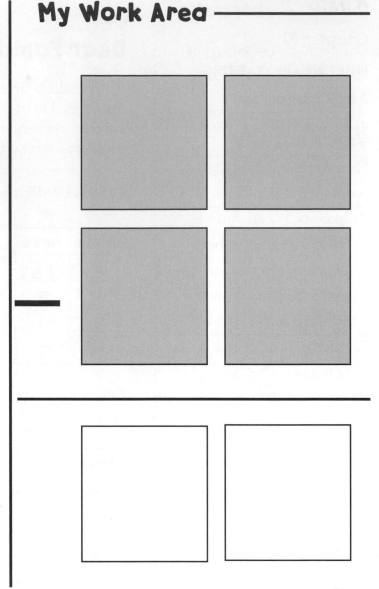

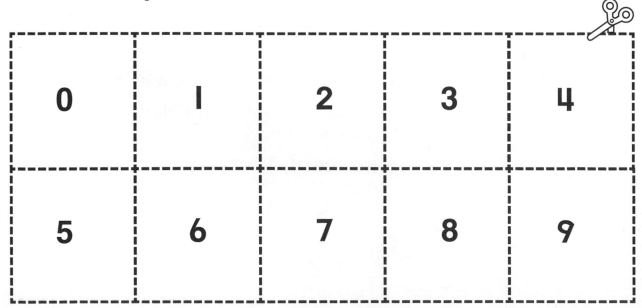

0	1	2	3	4
5	6	7	8	9

Name _____

2-Digit Subtraction

Subtract. Regroup when you need to.

1.

tens	ones
☐	☐
5	3
−	7

2.

tens	ones
☐	☐
4	8
−	6

3.

tens	ones
☐	☐
6	4
−	5

4.

tens	ones
☐	☐
2	9
− 1	3

5.

tens	ones
☐	☐
5	0
− 3	7

6.

tens	ones
☐	☐
4	3
− 2	8

7.

tens	ones
☐	☐
3	2
− 1	6

8.

tens	ones
☐	☐
7	6
− 5	2

9.

tens	ones
☐	☐
4	8
− 3	7

Subtract. Add to check.

10.   53
    −26   ☐
        + ☐
         ☐

11.   78
    −35   ☐
        + ☐
         ☐

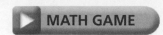

 Family Fun

Subtraction:
Right on Track

Materials small objects, such as pennies or paper clips (to use as game markers), paper, pencils

Directions

1. On separate slips of paper, write 2-digit subtraction problems like the sample problems on this page.
2. Take turns selecting a slip of paper and solving the problem.
3. Work together to check each player's subtraction. A player moves his or her game marker one space along the track for each correct answer.
4. Continue playing until all players reach the **Finish.**

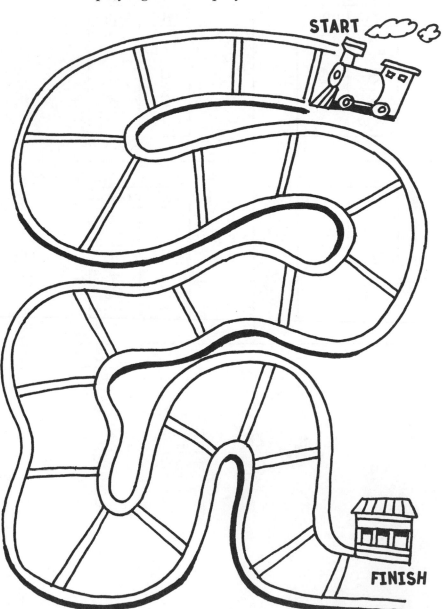

START

FINISH

Sample problems

1. 69
  −47

2. 53
  −47

3. 35
  −19

4. 41
  −28

5. 51
  −10

6. 63
  −28

7. 78
  −47

8. 84
  −36

9. 42
  −23

10. 64
  −47

Answers: 1. 22, 2. 6, 3. 16, 4. 13, 5. 41, 6. 35, 7. 31, 8. 48, 9. 19, 10. 17

FA42   Family Involvement Activities

WHAT WE ARE LEARNING

Practice 2-Digit Addition and
   Subtraction

VOCABULARY

Here is a vocabulary word
that we use in class:

Column addition

Addition of more than two
numbers
First add the ones. Then add
the tens.

Example:

$$
\begin{array}{r}
\overset{1}{5}4 \\
6 \\
+\,38 \\
\hline
98
\end{array}
$$

Name

Date

Dear Family,

Your child is continuing to add and subtract 2-digit
numbers. Sometimes these problems require
regrouping, and sometimes they do not. Your child is
also learning to use mental math to find sums and
differences. Here are examples of problems your child
is doing in class.

Use mental math to find sums or differences

What is $56 + 30$?
Count on by tens.
Say 56.
Count 66, 76, 86.

$56 + 30 = 86$

What is $56 - 30$?
Count back by tens.
Say 56.
Count 46, 36, 26.

$56 - 30 = 26$

What is $47 + 2$?
Count on by ones.
Say 47.
Count 48, 49.

$47 + 2 = 49$

What is $47 - 2$?
Count back by ones.
Say 47.
Count 46, 45.

$47 - 2 = 45$

Use pencil and paper

With regrouping:

$$
\begin{array}{r}
\overset{1}{}\;\; \\
3\;6 \\
+1\;7 \\
\hline
5\;3
\end{array}
\qquad
\begin{array}{r}
\overset{1}{}\;\; \\
3\;2 \\
7 \\
+1\;8 \\
\hline
5\;7
\end{array}
\qquad
\begin{array}{r}
\overset{4}{}\,\overset{13}{} \\
\cancel{5}\;\cancel{3} \\
-3\;8 \\
\hline
1\;5
\end{array}
$$

Without regrouping:

$$
\begin{array}{r}
2\;5 \\
+4\;3 \\
\hline
6\;8
\end{array}
\qquad
\begin{array}{r}
1\;3 \\
2\;1 \\
+3\;4 \\
\hline
6\;8
\end{array}
\qquad
\begin{array}{r}
5\;6 \\
-3\;4 \\
\hline
2\;2
\end{array}
$$

Help your child use the activity that follows to practice
adding 2-digit numbers.

Sincerely,

Subtracting 2-Digit Numbers

1. Solve the problem on each flower petal.

2. Cut out the vases and the flowers.

3. Which strategy did you use to solve the problems on each flower? Paste the flower on the stem in the vase that names the strategy.

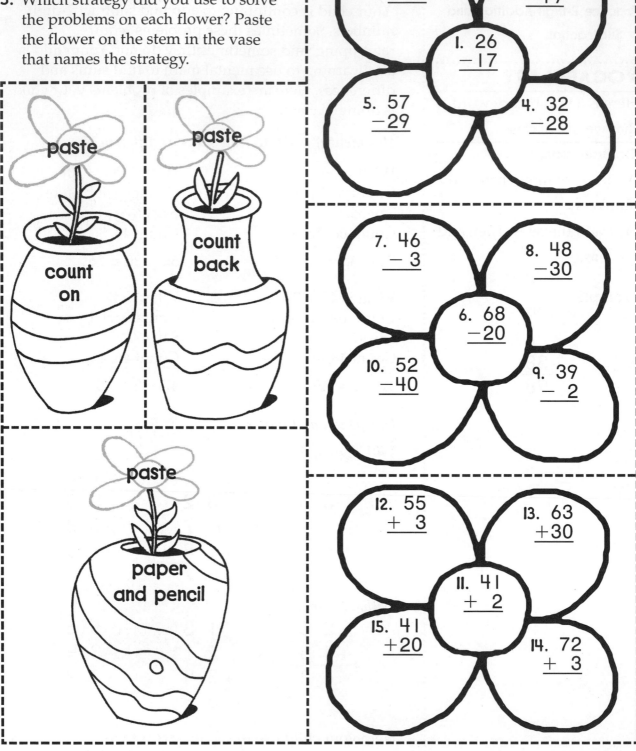

paste

count on

paste

count back

paste

paper and pencil

```
2.  46
   -18

3.  47
   -19

1.  26
   -17

5.  57
   -29

4.  32
   -28
```

```
7.  46
   - 3

8.  48
   -30

6.  68
   -20

10. 52
   -40

9.  39
   - 2
```

```
12. 55
   + 3

13. 63
   +30

11. 41
   + 2

15. 41
   +20

14. 72
   + 3
```

Answers: 1. 9; 2. 28; 3. 28; 4. 5; 5. 28; 6. 48; 7. 43; 8. 18; 9. 37; 10. 12; 11. 43; 12. 58; 13. 93; 14. 75; 15. 61; Paste flower 1–5 on the *paper and pencil* vase. Paste flower 6–10 on the *count back* vase. Paste flower 11–15 on the *count on* vase.

Practice 2-Digit Addition and Subtraction

Add or subtract.

1. $\begin{array}{r} 17 \\ + 14 \\ \hline \end{array}$ □

2. $\begin{array}{r} 54 \\ + 38 \\ \hline \end{array}$ □

3. $\begin{array}{r} 63 \\ + 25 \\ \hline \end{array}$ □

4. $\begin{array}{r} 29 \\ + 41 \\ \hline \end{array}$ □

5. $\begin{array}{r} 80 \\ + 13 \\ \hline \end{array}$ □

6. $\begin{array}{r} 15 \\ + 72 \\ \hline \end{array}$ □

7. $\begin{array}{r} 48 \\ 27 \\ + 21 \\ \hline \end{array}$ □

8. $\begin{array}{r} 16 \\ 53 \\ + 12 \\ \hline \end{array}$ □

9. $\begin{array}{r} 48 \\ - 22 \\ \hline \end{array}$ □

10. $\begin{array}{r} 31 \\ - 27 \\ \hline \end{array}$ □

11. $\begin{array}{r} 49 \\ - 31 \\ \hline \end{array}$ □

12. $\begin{array}{r} 52 \\ - 38 \\ \hline \end{array}$ □

13. $\begin{array}{r} 35 \\ - 16 \\ \hline \end{array}$ □

14. $\begin{array}{r} 57 \\ - 32 \\ \hline \end{array}$ □

15. $\begin{array}{r} 86 \\ - 7 \\ \hline \end{array}$ □

16. $\begin{array}{r} 37 \\ - 19 \\ \hline \end{array}$ □

17. $\begin{array}{r} 38 \\ + 47 \\ \hline \end{array}$ □

18. $\begin{array}{r} 63 \\ + 22 \\ \hline \end{array}$ □

19. $\begin{array}{r} 58 \\ - 22 \\ \hline \end{array}$ □

20. $\begin{array}{r} 73 \\ + 9 \\ \hline \end{array}$ □

21. $\begin{array}{r} 63 \\ - 21 \\ \hline \end{array}$ □

22. $\begin{array}{r} 28 \\ + 37 \\ \hline \end{array}$ □

23. $\begin{array}{r} 42 \\ - 28 \\ \hline \end{array}$ □

24. $\begin{array}{r} 18 \\ + 5 \\ \hline \end{array}$ □

Family Fun **Sort the** Mail

1. Take turns solving the problems.
2. Draw lines to match the sums and differences to the addresses on the houses. Have each player use a different-colored crayon.
3. Circle the houses that match more than one answer. What is the same about those houses?

1. 98 − 23	2. 63 + 8	3. 92 − 19	4. 39 + 38	5. 82 − 5	6. 76 + 3

7. 54 + 26	8. 90 − 19	9. 59 + 16	10. 66 + 7	11. 82 − 3	12. 44 + 38

Want to do more? Help your child think of other problems with sums and differences that match the numbers on the houses. Write the problems on slips of paper and place them by the appropriate houses.

Answers: 1. 75; **2.** 71; **3.** 73; **4.** 77; **5.** 77; **6.** 79; **7.** 80; **8.** 71; **9.** 75; **10.** 73; **11.** 79; **12.** 82; The circled houses have odd numbers.

HARCOURT MATH

GRADE 2

Chapter 12

WHAT WE ARE LEARNING

Counting Money

....

VOCABULARY

Here are the vocabulary words we use in class:

Half dollar

A coin worth 50¢

 or

One dollar

A bill worth $1.00 or 100¢

or

Decimal point A dot to separate dollars from cents in money

Example: $3.29

Dollar sign A symbol ($) written before a number to show money

---

Name _____

Date _____

Dear Family,

Your child is learning to count on to find the total amount in a group of coins, to understand the values of a half dollar and dollar, and to add money. Here is information about money that your child is using in class.

Counting coin combinations

To count your coins:

1. Place the coins in order from greatest value to least value.

2. Count on by using the value of each coin.

25¢, 35¢, 45¢, 50¢, 51¢

Identify values

 or   This is a half dollar. It has a value of 50¢.

or

{ This is a one-dollar bill.
It has a value of $1.00 or 100¢.

Add money

Add the ones.   25¢
Add the tens.   +36¢
Write ¢.   61¢

Help your child use these strategies and the exercises that follow to practice identifying coins and counting coin combinations up to $1.00.

Sincerely,

Counting Coin Combinations

1. Cut out the coins on the page or use real coins.

2. Have your child identify the name and value of each coin.

3. Now use the chart. Read each amount.

4. In the space provided, place coins to show the amount.

5. There is more than one way to make each amount. Help your child show another coin combination for each amount.

Tip: Save the paper coins in a self-sealing bag for use with other activities.

Amount	Coins Used
35¢	
17¢	
65¢	
88¢	

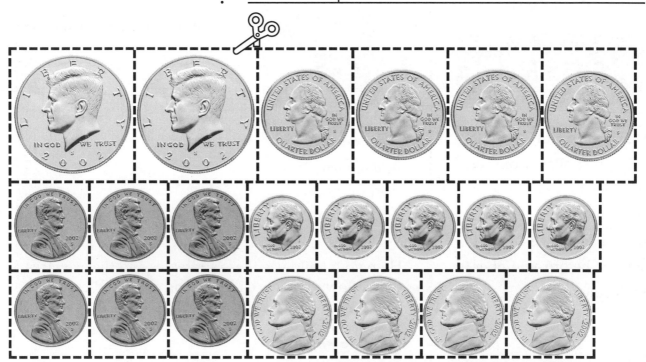

Answers: Answers will vary. One possible coin combination is given for each value. 35¢: 1 quarter, 1 dime; 17¢: 1 dime, 1 nickel, 2 pennies; 65¢: 1 half-dollar, 1 dime, 1 nickel; 88¢: 1 half-dollar, 1 quarter, 1 dime, 3 pennies

Name _____

Counting Money

Count on to find the total amount.

1.

____ ¢   ____ ¢   ____ ¢   ____ ¢   ____ ¢   ____ ¢   [ ] ¢

2.

____ ¢   ____ ¢   ____ ¢   ____ ¢   ____ ¢   [ ] ¢

Show a way to make $1.00. Draw coins.

3.

_____

Add. Regroup if you need to.

4.　 38¢　　5.　 13¢　　6.　 23¢　　7.　　5¢
　 +12¢　　　 +5¢　　　 +49¢　　　 +25¢

8.　 20¢　　9.　 57¢　　10.　 45¢　　11.　 35¢
　 +36¢　　　 +23¢　　　 +15¢　　　 +28¢

Answers: 1. 25¢, 35¢, 45¢, 46¢, 47¢, 48¢; **2.** 25¢, 50¢, 55¢, 60¢, 61¢; **3.** Possible answer is 2 quarters and 5 dimes; **4.** 50¢; **5.** 18¢; **6.** 72¢; **7.** 30¢; **8.** 56¢; **9.** 80¢; **10.** 60¢; **11.** 63¢

Family Involvement Activities　FA49

Family Fun Let's Go Shopping!

Materials

Real coins or the paper coins from page FA48

For each player, a game marker, such as a bean or button

Paper and pencil

Directions

1. The first player puts a penny in his or her cupped hands, shakes the penny, and lets it fall to the table.

   - Move 1 space if the penny shows heads.
   - Move 2 spaces if the penny shows tails.

2. Follow the directions on the game-board spaces.

3. If you land on a space showing a price tag, purchase the item. Show a coin combination equal to the price of the item. Keep a list of all items you purchase.

4. Take turns moving along the game board. Play continues until all players leave the store. The player with more purchases is the winner.

WHAT WE ARE LEARNING
Using Money

....

VOCABULARY

Here is a vocabulary word that we use in class:

Change The difference between the price of an item and the amount you give the clerk

"If you give the clerk 30¢ for the ball, you get 3¢ change."

Name _____

Date _____

Dear Family,

Your child is continuing to learn about money. Here are money skills your child is learning:

Show a value using the fewest coins

Your child is learning that in order to show a value using the fewest number of coins, he or she needs to use coins with the greatest value possible.

Compare amounts

Your child is learning to compare two amounts and to compare an amount to a price.

60¢ > 45¢

If you have 60¢, you can buy a 53¢ toy cat.

Make change

The cat costs 53¢. You give the clerk 60¢. How much change do you get back?

Say 53¢. Count on: 54¢, 55¢, 60¢.
Your change is 2 pennies and 1 nickel, or 7¢.

Help your child use the activity that follows to practice working with money.

Sincerely,

Modeling Money

1. Cut out and use the coins on this page or use real coins.
2. Use half dollars and quarters to buy each item. Use dimes, nickels, and pennies to show the change.
3. Complete the chart.

Buy this item.	How much change do you get back? Draw the coins. Write the amount.
1. 38¢	_____ ¢
2. 92¢	_____ ¢
3. 85¢	_____ ¢

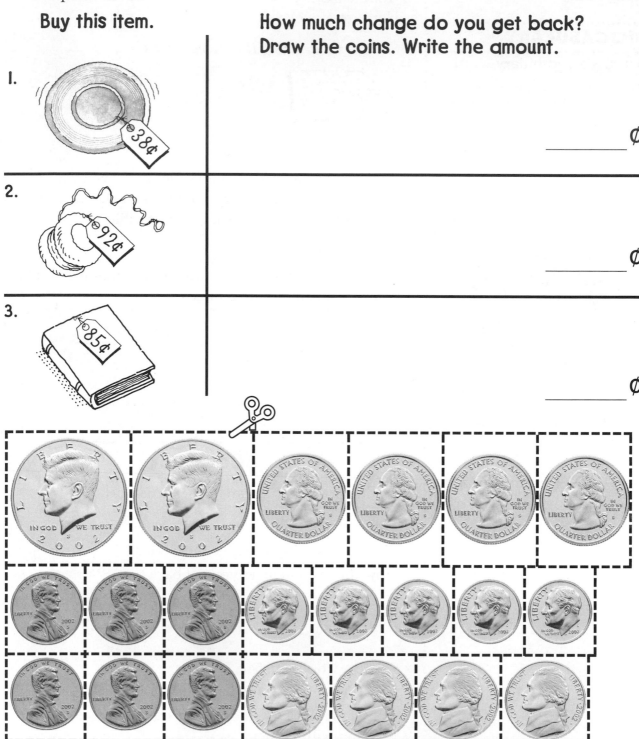

Name_____

Using Money

Write the amount. Then use the fewest coins to show the same amount. Draw and label the coins.

1.

_____ ¢

[blank box]

2.

_____ ¢

[blank box]

Count on from the price to find the change.

3. You have 50¢. You buy

47¢, _____, _____, _____

Your change is _____.

4. You have 25¢. You buy

17¢, _____, _____, _____, _____

Your change is _____.

Family Fun

1. Cut out the money squares at the bottom of the page, and place them in a bag.
2. Take turns selecting a money square and placing it above an item you want to buy.
3. On a separate sheet of paper, write a subtraction problem to find the amount of money you would have left after buying it. Circle that amount.
4. Place the money square back in the bag. Continue until each person has had a chance to buy at least five items.

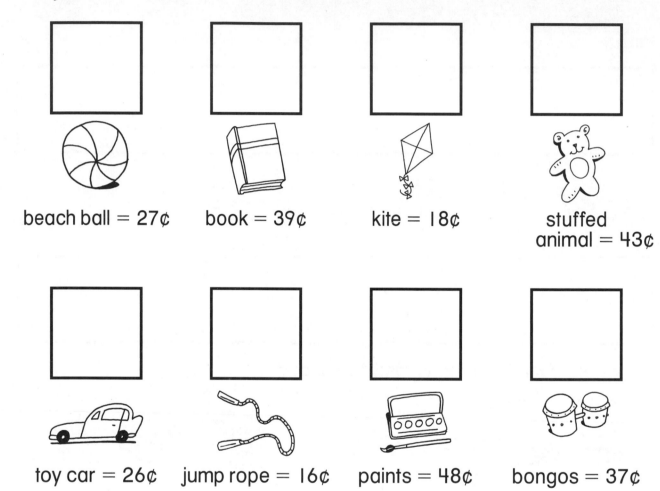

beach ball = 27¢ book = 39¢ kite = 18¢ stuffed animal = 43¢

toy car = 26¢ jump rope = 16¢ paints = 48¢ bongos = 37¢

Want to do more?

Help your child create an addition problem to add up the amount of money left over from his or her purchases. Have your child decide which item or items he or she could buy using the leftover amount.

| 50¢ | 55¢ | 60¢ | 65¢ | 70¢ | 75¢ | 80¢ |

HARCOURT MATH
GRADE 2

Chapter 14

WHAT WE ARE LEARNING
Telling Time

VOCABULARY

Here are the vocabulary words we use in class:

Minute A unit used to measure time. There are 60 minutes in one hour.

Hour Another unit used to measure time. There are 24 hours in one day.

Half-hour The middle point of an hour. There are 30 minutes in a half-hour.

Dear Family,

Your child is learning to tell time. Here are some things your child is learning about time.

Telling time

5 minutes

It takes 5 minutes for the minute hand to move to each number on the clock. When the minute hand points to 1, it is 5 minutes after the hour.

Different ways to say time

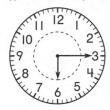

1. 6:15

2. 15 minutes after 6

3. quarter past 6

1. Say the hour and the number of minutes after the hour.

2. Say the number of minutes after the hour.

3. Say *quarter past* the hour when it is 15 minutes after the hour.

1. 7:45

2. 15 minutes before 8

3. quarter to 8

1. Say the hour and the number of minutes after the hour.

2. Say the number of minutes before the next hour.

3. Say *quarter to* the hour when it is 15 minutes before the next hour.

Help your child use these strategies and the activity that follows to practice telling time.

Sincerely,

Telling Time

1. Cut out the clock, the clock hands, and the time phrases. You may want to glue this paper to a medium size box, such as a cereal box, first.

2. Place the minute hand and then the hour hand on the clock so the black circles are on top of one another.

3. Push a fastener, such as a pushpin or a brad, through the black circles to secure the hands to the clock.

   Use caution when handling sharp objects.

4. Take turns selecting a time phrase, reading the phrase, and moving the clock's hands to show that time.

5. You can vary the activity by showing a time on the clock and having the other players name the time.

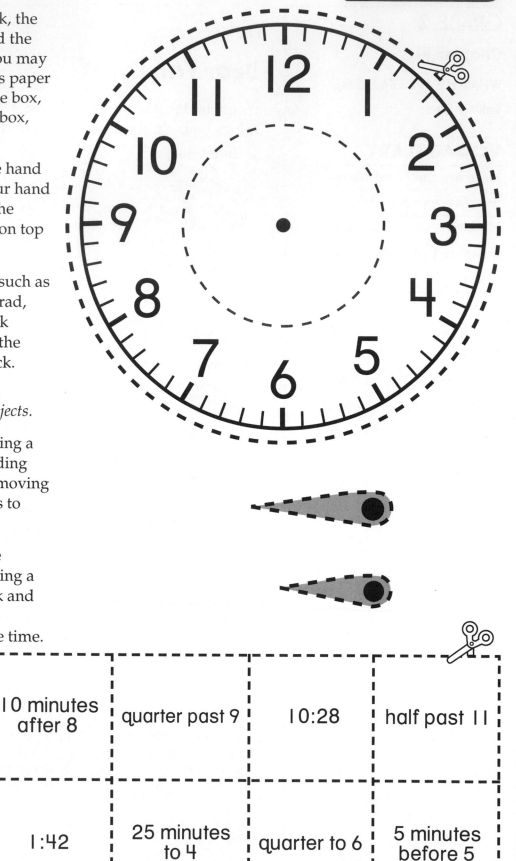

5:25	10 minutes after 8	quarter past 9	10:28	half past 11
40 minutes after 2	1:42	25 minutes to 4	quarter to 6	5 minutes before 5

Name _____

Telling Time

Draw the minute hand. Write the time.

1.   6 o'clock

_____ : _____

2.   10 o'clock

_____ : _____

3.   half past 4

_____ : _____

4.   two thirty

_____ : _____

5.   quarter to 8

_____ : _____

6.   quarter past 2

_____ : _____

Write the time.

7.

_____ : _____

8.

_____ : _____

9.

_____ : _____

Family Involvement Activities   FA57

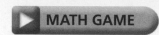

Family Fun Bingo Time!

1. Make bingo cards like the one on this page. Make two cards for each player.

2. Have players write a different time in each box on one of their cards. Then have players copy those exact times onto their second cards.

3. Have players cut apart the boxes on their second cards and place the boxes in a bowl.

4. Identify one player to be the caller. This person selects a box from the bowl and shows that time on the clock from page FA56.

5. Players look for that time on their bingo cards. Players who can find that time place game markers, such as paper clips or paper scraps, on that time on their bingo cards.

6. When a player has three markers in a row or column, the player calls out "Bingo Time!" He or she reads the time in each box while removing the game markers.

7. To begin a new game, put all time boxes back in the bowl and clear all game markers from the bingo cards.

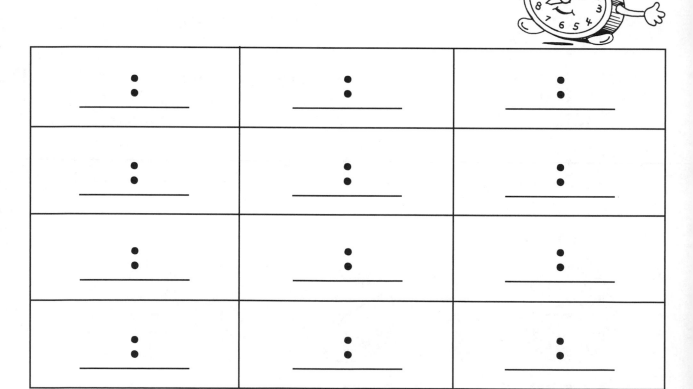

Understanding Time

VOCABULARY

Here are the vocabulary words we use in class:

Calendar A table that shows the days, weeks, and months of a year.

Month There are 12 months in one year: *January, February, March, April, May, June, July, August, September, October, November,* and *December.*

Year There are 12 months in one year.

Day There are 24 hours in one day.

Date The day of the month; for example, August 2 or November 28

Week There are 7 days in one week: *Sunday, Monday, Tuesday, Wednesday, Thursday, Friday, and Saturday.*

Name _____

Date

Dear Family,

Your child is learning about time relationships.

Reading a calendar
Your child is using a calendar to talk about time relationships and to write dates. The third Friday is May 19. After May comes June.

May						
Sunday	Monday	Tuesday	Wednesday	Thursday	Friday	Saturday
	1	2	3	4	5	6
7	8	9	10	11	12	13
14	15	16	17	18	19	20
21	22	23	24	25	26	27
28	29	30	31			

month — day — week — date

Comparing units of time
Your child is learning to compare time using the words *more than, less than,* or *the same as.*

40 days is more than 1 month.

8 months is less than 1 year.

7 days is the same as 1 week.

Estimating time
Your child is estimating how long events take in minutes, hours, days, weeks, months, and years. For example, your child might estimate that it takes about 4 minutes to brush his or her teeth and about 1 hour to play a game.

Help your child use the activity that follows to practice reading a calendar.

Sincerely,

Reading a Calendar

February

Sunday	Monday	Tuesday	Wednesday	Thursday	Friday	Saturay
	1	2	3	4	5	6
7	8	9	10	11	12	13
♡ 14	15	16	17	18	19	20
21	22	23	24	25	26	27
28						

Ask questions such as the following to talk about the calendar. If you have a calendar at home, ask similar questions about the month you are in.

1. What is the name of the month?
2. What day is February 9th?
3. How many Thursdays are in this month?
4. How many holidays are identified?
5. Why is there a heart on February 14th?
6. On what day will the next month begin?

Answers: 1. February; **2.** Tuesday; **3.** 4; **4.** 3; **5.** To remind you that day is Valentines Day; **6.** Monday

Name _____

Understanding Time

Use the calendar to answer the questions.

1. What is the date two weeks after June 7?

   _____

2. What is the date of the second Saturday?

   _____

3. What is the date one day after June 30?

   _____

June						
Sunday	Monday	Tuesday	Wednesday	Thursday	Friday	Saturday
		1	2	3	4	5
6	7	8	9	10	11	12
13	14	15	16	17	18	19
20	21	22	23	24	25	26
27	28	29	30			

Complete the sentences.

Write *more than, less than,* or *the same as.*

4. It took 3 weeks for Jim's plant to flower. This is

   _____ 1 month.

5. Jenny read her book for 7 days. This is

   _____ 1 week.

Find the reasonable answers.

Circle the amount of time that makes sense.

6. eat breakfast

20 minutes   20 hours

7. read 5 pages

15 weeks   15 minutes

Family Fun Equal Time

1. Cut out the time-phrase cards below.
2. Mix them, and place them face down in 4 rows of 4.
3. The first player turns over 2 cards. If they show equivalent amounts of time on them, such as *7 days* and *1 week*, then the player keeps the cards and takes another turn. If the times are not equivalent, the cards are returned to their original, face-down positions, and it is the next player's turn.
4. Continue until all of the cards have been matched. The player with more cards is the winner.

60 seconds	1 minute	7 days	1 week
28, 29, 30, or 31 days	1 month	52 weeks	1 year
60 minutes	1 hour	24 hours	1 day
12 months	1 year	1 half-hour	30 minutes

Answers: 60 seconds = 1 minute; 30 minutes = $\frac{1}{2}$ hour; 60 minutes = 1 hour; 24 hours = 1 day; 7 days = 1 week; 52 weeks = 1 year; 28, 29, 30, or 31 days = 1 month; 12 months = 1 year

HARCOURT MATH
GRADE 2
Chapter 16

WHAT WE ARE LEARNING
Interpret Tables and Graphs

VOCABULARY

Here are the vocabulary words we use in class:

Bar graph A graph that uses bars to show data.

Range The difference between the greatest number and the least number in a set of data.

Median The middle number in an ordered set of data.

Mode The number found most often in a set of data.

Grid The horizontal and vertical lines on a map.

Point An exact position or location.

Line graph A graph that uses a line to show how something changes over time.

Name _____

Date

Dear Family,

Your child is learning how to interpret data in tables and graphs, including bar graphs and line graphs. Here is how your child might answer questions about this bar graph.

FAVORITE FRUIT

Apple	Orange	Banana	Pear

(bar graph: Apple = 8, Orange = 3, Banana = 6, Pear = 2; y-axis 0–10)

1. An apple is the favorite fruit of how many children?

   To answer this question, your child must find the column for apple.
   Then your child finds the top of the shaded bar and identifies the number to the left of it. (8)
   Your child might confirm the number by counting the number of shaded boxes.
   Your child uses this information to answer the question: *An apple is the favorite fruit of 8 children.*

2. How many children in all chose oranges or pears?

   To answer this question, your child finds out how many children chose oranges (3) and how many chose pears (2).
   Then your child must add the numbers: 3 + 2 = 5.
   Together, 5 children chose oranges or pears.

Your child is also learning how to find the range, median, and mode of data.

Use the activities that follow to help your child make and answer questions about tables and graphs.

Sincerely,

Family Involvement Activities   FA63

Make a Line Graph

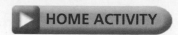

A line graph is a graph that uses a line to show how something changes over time. Use the activity below to help your child practice reading a line graph.

1. With your child, find the weather forecast for the next five days.

2. Help your child plot the daily high temperature and read the graph.

3. Finally, have your child explain the completed graph.

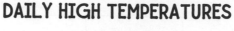

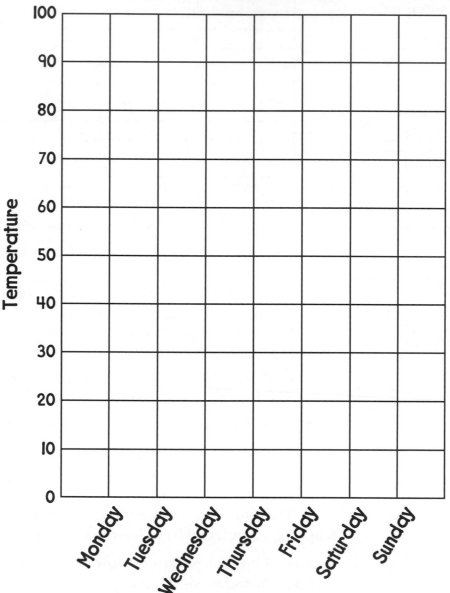

Name _____

Interpret Tables and Graphs

Make a bar graph to show how many of each coin there are.

Number of Coins			
6			
5			
4			
3			
2			
1			
0			
Pennies	**Nickels**	**Dimes**	**Quarters**

Use the bar graph to answer the questions.

1. How many dimes are there? ☐

2. How many pennies and nickels are there in all? ☐

3. How many more dimes than quarters are there? ☐

4. How many more pennies than dimes are there? ☐

Family Fun

Treasure Hunt

1. Cut out the cards to the right. Mix up the cards and place them face down on the table.

2. Players take turns selecting a card and locating the point on the grid.

3. Once a player locates the point, he or she records the number of coins in the treasure chest on the score card below the grid.

4. Players total their scores after five rounds. The player with the highest score wins.

(6,5)	(3,2)
(4,4)	(1,5)
(2,3)	(6,3)
(1,1)	(5,6)
(3,6)	(5,1)

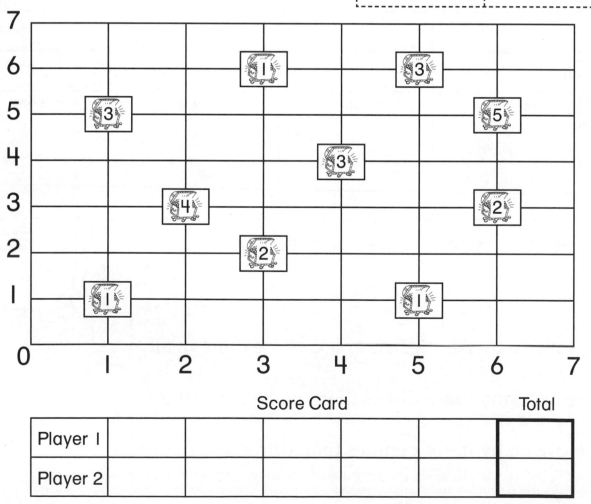

Score Card | Total

Player 1						
Player 2						

FA66**Family Involvement Activities**

HARCOURT MATH
GRADE 2

Chapter 17

WHAT WE ARE LEARNING

Probability

VOCABULARY

Here are the vocabulary words we use in class:

Outcome A possible result of an experiment.

Event Something that happens.

Certain Having every chance of happening.

Impossible Having no chance of happening.

Likely Having a good chance of happening.

Unlikely Not having a good chance of happening.

Equally likely Having the same chance of happening.

Dear Family,

Your child is learning about probability. In class we are learning how to recognize possible outcomes and to predict future outcomes.

An **outcome** is the result of an event. If you toss a coin, the possible outcomes are heads and tails. Since they have an equal chance of happening, the outcomes heads and tails are **equally likely**.

Now look at the spinner below. Which outcome is **more likely**, spinning a 1 or a 2? Which outcome is **more unlikely**?

It is more likely that the spinner will land on 1. It is less likely that the spinner will land on 2.

An event is **certain** if it always happens. It is certain that the spinner will land on 1 or 2. An event is **impossible** if it cannot happen. It is impossible that the spinner will land on 3 because 3 is not on the spinner.

Use **most likely** and **least likely** when there are more than two possible outcomes of an event.

Help your child use the activities that follow to practice identifying and predicting outcomes.

Sincerely,

Interpreting Outcomes

1. Use the spinner below. Use a pencil and paper clip as a pointer.

2. Spin 10 times.

3. Write D (DOG) or C (CAT) in the chart to record each outcome.

Spin	1	2	3	4	5	6	7	8	9	10
Outcome										

4. Answer the questions below using the chart.

What are the possible outcomes for this spinner? _____

How many times was DOG the outcome? _____

How many times was CAT the outcome? _____

Predict. If you used the spinner 5 more times, which outcome do you think you would spin more often? _____

Spin 5 more times. How closely did the outcome match your prediction? _____

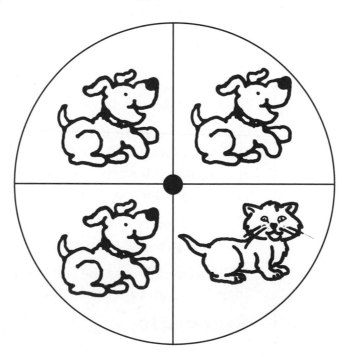

Name _____

Probability

Write *likely* or *unlikely* to tell the chance of pulling a white cube or a gray cube from the bag.

1.

Use the tally table to answer the question.

2. Amy pulled some crayons from a box. She recorded the outcomes of 10 pulls to see which color was more likely to be pulled. What does the data show is the more likely color to be pulled?

_____

Pulls of Crayons from the Box	
Color	Tally
Orange	ЖНТ III
Yellow	II

Use the spinner to answer the questions.

3. What are the possible outcomes of using this spinner?

_____

4. Which outcome is least likely?

_____

5. Which outcomes are equally likely?

_____

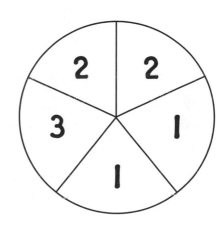

Family Fun

What's in the Bag?

1. Color and cut out the circles on this page (3 red, 3 blue, and 3 green).

2. Player 1 selects 6 of the circles and places them into a small paper bag without Player 2 seeing them. The bag must contain at least 1 red, 1 blue, and 1 green circle.

3. Player 2 reaches into the bag, pulls out one circle, and then records the color in the tally table below.

4. Player 1 returns the circle to the bag and shakes the bag.

5. Repeat steps 3 and 4 until Player 2 has recorded 10 colors in the tally table. Player 2 then must try to guess the color combination in the bag, based on the data collected in the tally table.

6. Player 1 and Player 2 then switch roles.

7. The player who correctly guesses the color combination wins the game. If both players guess correctly, or if neither player guesses correctly, play another round.

Color Red	Color Red	Color Red
Color Blue	Color Blue	Color Blue
Color Green	Color Green	Color Green

Pull	1	2	3	4	5	6	7	8	9	10
Color										

Player 1

Pull	1	2	3	4	5	6	7	8	9	10
Color										

Player 2

WHAT WE ARE LEARNING

Plane Shapes

VOCABULARY

Here are the vocabulary words we use in class:

Plane shapes Shapes in a plane that are formed by lines that are curved, straight, or both.

Square

Rectangle

Triangle

Hexagon

Trapezoid

Parallelogram

Circle

Name

Date

Dear Family,

Your child is learning about plane shapes. Here is a summary of our class discussions.

Some plane shapes have **sides**, which are straight edges, and **corners**, which are where two sides meet.

A square has 4 sides and 4 corners.

A rectangle has 4 sides and 4 corners.

A triangle has 3 sides and 3 corners.

A hexagon has 6 sides and 6 corners.

A trapezoid has 4 sides and 4 corners.

A parallelogram has 4 sides and 4 corners.

A circle has 0 sides and 0 corners.

You can make new shapes by combining shapes

or by separating shapes.

Use the activity that follows to explore plane shapes with your child.

Sincerely,

Identify the Shapes

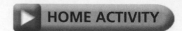

1. Color the squares blue.
2. Color the rectangles green.
3. Color the triangles yellow.
4. Color the hexagons orange.
5. Color the trapezoids purple.
6. Color the circles brown.

Name _____

Plane Shapes

Write how many sides and corners each shape has.

1.

☐sides ☐corners

2.
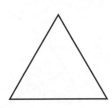
☐sides ☐corners

3.
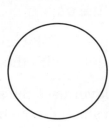
☐sides ☐corners

Color the two shapes in each row that can
be put together to make the first shape.

4.

5.
  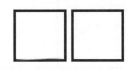

6.
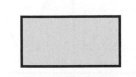 

7.
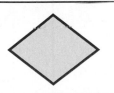 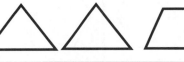 

8.
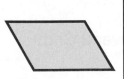   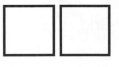 

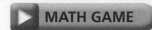

With Shapes

1. Use a pencil point and paper clip as a pointer with the spinner.

2. One player uses the spinner and finds a shape in the tic-tac-toe grid that has the same number of sides as the number the spinner lands on.

3. The player then colors the shape and the next player takes a turn.

4. The winner is the first player who fills a row, column, or diagonal.

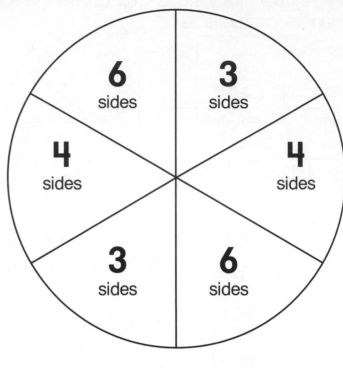

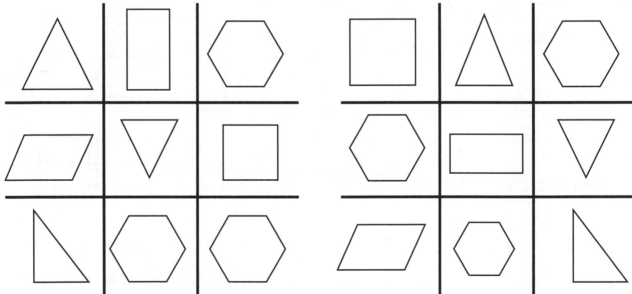

Player 1 Grid   Player 2 Grid

HARCOURT MATH

GRADE 2

Chapter 19

WHAT WE ARE LEARNING

Solid Figures

....

VOCABULARY

Here are the vocabulary words we use in class:

Solid figures Figures that have length, width, and height.

Rectangular prism

Sphere

Cone

Cylinder

Cube

Pyramid

Name _____

Date _____

Dear Family,

Your child is identifying solid figures and the plane shapes that form the faces of the solid figures. Here is a summary of our class discussions.

A solid figure might have a **face**, which is a flat surface, an **edge**, which is where two faces meet, and a **corner**, which is where the edges meet.

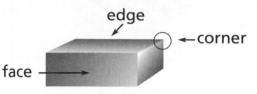

A rectangular prism has 6 faces, 12 edges, and 8 corners.

A sphere has 0 faces, 0 edges, and 0 corners.

A cone has 1 face, 1 edge, and 0 corners.

A cylinder has 2 faces, 2 edges, and 0 corners.

A cube has 6 faces, 12 edges, and 8 corners.

A pyramid has 5 faces, 8 edges, and 5 corners.

Help your child use the activity that follows to practice identifying solid figures.

Sincerely,

Finding Solid Figures

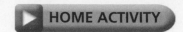

1. Find two examples in your house of each solid figure on this page.
2. Write the names of the items you find in the space provided.

Solid	Example	Example

Tip: Examples of solid figures can often be found in the kitchen. Possible examples: rectangular prism = cereal box, cube = tissue box, sphere = orange, cylinder = paper-towel roll, cone = ice-cream cone.

Solid Figures

Draw lines to match each solid figure to the shape of its face.
Some solid figures match more than one plane shape.
Some solid figures have no matches.

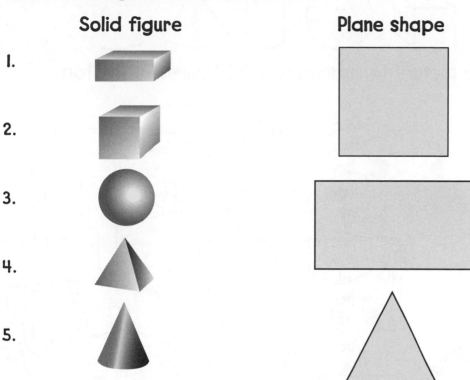

Solid figure   Plane shape

1.

2.

3.

4.

5.

Each of these solid figures is sitting on an ink pad.
Which shape will each figure make? Draw the shape.

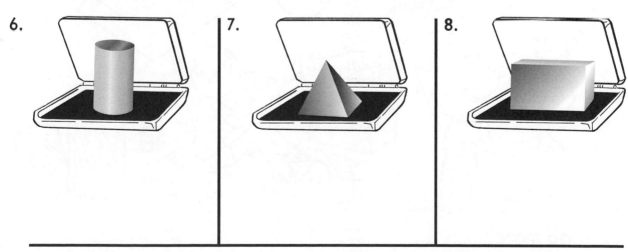

6.   7.   8.

Family Fun — Shapes at the Beach

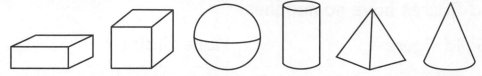

Color each solid figure a different color.

Color objects in the picture to match the solid figures at the top of the page.

Want to do more?

Look through picture books together to identify solid figures. Which solid figures do you find most often? Which do you find least often? Why do you think that is?

WHAT WE ARE LEARNING

Spatial Sense

VOCABULARY

Here are the vocabulary words we use in class:

Congruent Figures that have the same size and shape.

Symmetry When one half of a figure looks like the mirror image of the other half of a figure.

Flip, turn, slide

Start with a shape:

You still have the same shape if you **flip** it,

turn it,

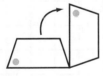

or **slide** it.

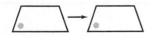

Name _____

Date _____

Dear Family,

Your child is learning about congruence, symmetry, and moving shapes. Congruent figures are the same size and shape.

The two triangles are congruent.

The two squares are not congruent.

A line of symmetry divides a figure into two congruent figures.

The dashed line in each figure is a line of symmetry.

Your child is also learning about moving shapes by sliding, flipping, and turning them.

Help your child use the activity that follows to explore and develop a sense of spatial relationships.

Sincerely,

Turns, Flips, and Slides

1. Use the grid on this page.

2. Have your child cut out the plane shapes on the bottom of this page.
Ask him or her these questions, *How many sides are there? How many corners are there?*

3. After all shapes are cut out, take turns selecting a shape and tracing it on the grid.

4. Then move the shape by turning it, flipping it, or sliding it.

5. Trace how the plane shape looks in the new position on the grid.

6. Talk about what happens to the "x" on each shape after you flip it, turn it, and slide it.

Tip: Your child might enjoy creating his or her own shapes to turn, flip, and slide.

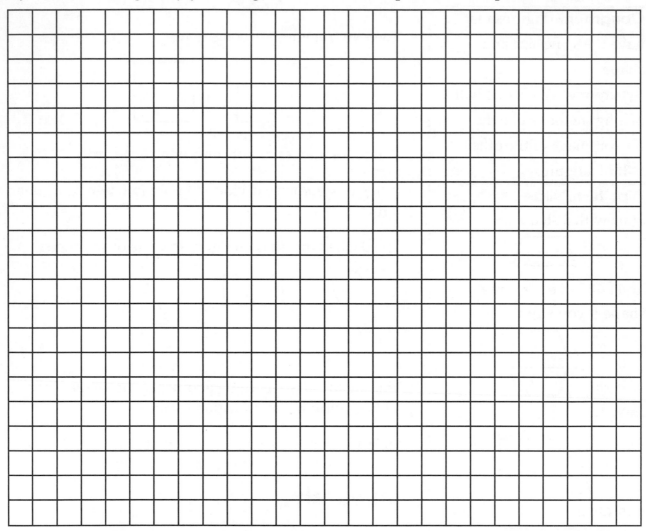

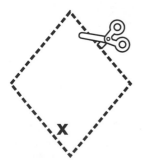 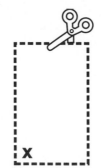 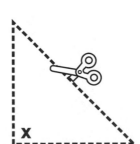 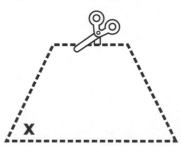

FA80 **Family Involvement Activities**

Name _____

Spatial Sense

Are the figures congruent? Circle Yes or No.

1.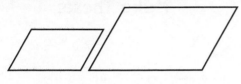

   Yes   No

2.

   Yes   No

3.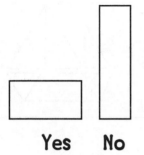

   Yes   No

4.

   Yes   No

Draw a line of symmetry. The two parts will be congruent.

5.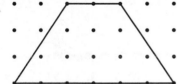

6.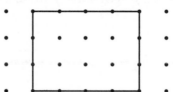

Write the word that names the move.

7.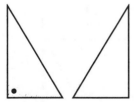

   _____

8.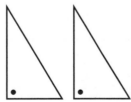

   _____

9.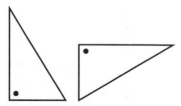

   _____

Family Fun   Shape Sculptures!

1. Cut out the plane shapes at the bottom of this page. Point out any shapes that are congruent.

2. You can make more sets if you like. You might want to use poster board rather than paper.

3. Use the shapes to make the pictures on this page. The number next to each picture tells how many pieces were used to make it. (Since there is more than one way to make each picture, you might be able to use a different number of pieces.)

4. Store your shape pieces in a self-sealing bag for safekeeping. Then you can use them again and again.

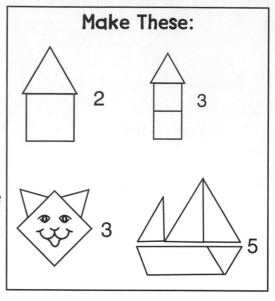

Make These:

Want to do more?   Use the plane shapes to create your own pictures. Trace the outline of the completed picture, then remove the plane shapes. Ask a family member to use the plane shapes to recreate your picture.

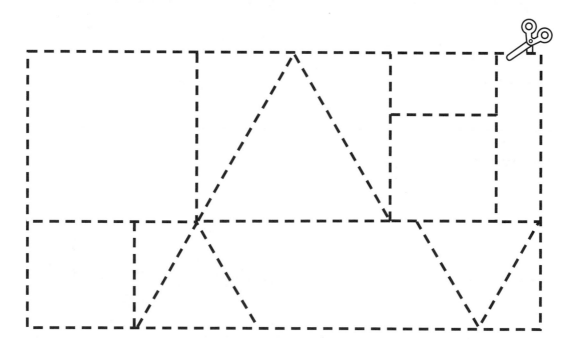

Answers: House = triangle on square; **arrow** = two squares and a triangle; **cat's face** = square turned as diamond and triangle on either side to create ears; **boat** = triangle next to parallelogram, with three triangles on top.

FA82   Family Involvement Activities

WHAT WE ARE LEARNING

Patterns

VOCABULARY

Here is a vocabulary word we use in class:

Pattern unit The part of a pattern that repeats over and over

Name _____

Date _____

Dear Family,

Your child is learning to describe, extend, and create patterns. Here is a summary of our class discussions.

Describing Patterns
A pattern is something that repeats over and over. Patterns can be found everywhere. They can be found in shapes, numbers, and colors.

This is a pattern:

The pattern unit is what repeats over and over in a pattern:

Extending Patterns
You can extend the pattern by continuing with more pattern units.

Creating Patterns
You can use shapes from one pattern to make a new pattern.

Pattern 1

Pattern 2

Help your child use these strategies and the activity that follows to practice patterns.

Sincerely,

Making Patterns with Shapes

1. Cut out the shapes at the bottom of the page.
2. Use the shapes to correct the mistakes in the three patterns below by placing the correct shape over the incorrect shape.
3. Use the remaining shapes to create a new pattern.

New Pattern:

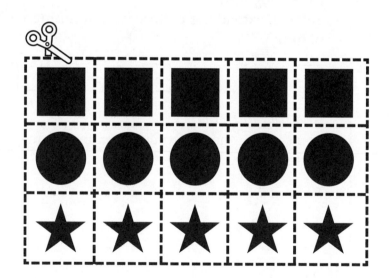

Name _____

Patterns

1. Draw to continue the pattern.

---

2. Circle the pattern unit in the pattern.

5 7 9 5 7 9 5 7 9 5 7 9

---

3. Use the same shapes to make a new pattern. Draw the new pattern.

---

4. Circle the mistake in the pattern. Draw the correct pattern.

Family Fun

Amazing Patterns

1. Go to the beginning of the maze and describe the pattern.
2. Follow the pattern through the maze to get to the finish line.
3. Create a pattern and make your own maze.

Start

Finish

HARCOURT MATH

GRADE 2

Chapter 22

WHAT WE ARE LEARNING

Customary Measurement:
   Length and Temperature

VOCABULARY

Here are the vocabulary words we use in class:

Inch A unit to measure short lengths

This part of a thumb is about 1 inch long.

Foot A unit to measure longer lengths

A three-ring notebook is about 1 foot tall.

Yard A unit to measure longer lengths. A door knob is about 1 yard from the floor.

Temperature A measure of heat or cold given in degrees Fahrenheit (°F).

Name _____

Date _____

Dear Family,

Your child is learning about ways to measure. Here is a summary of our class discussions.

How to Measure Length

1. Identify the units of measure you will use: nonstandard, such as paper clips, or standard, such as inches, feet, or yards.
2. Estimate how many units long the object is.
3. Identify the point where you will start measuring and the point where you will stop measuring.
4. Use a measuring tool to measure the object.
5. Be sure your measuring tool is placed exactly at the start point.

For example, this is how to measure this comb.

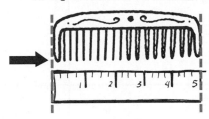

Temperature

Temperature tells how hot or cold something is. We use degrees Fahrenheit to measure temperature on a thermometer.

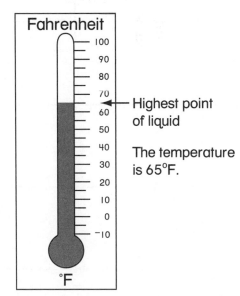

Help your child use the activity that follows to practice measuring.

Sincerely,

Practice Measuring

1. Cut out the rulers on page FA91.
2. Find an object you want to measure. Write its name in the chart.
3. Write the unit you will use to measure the object.
4. Estimate how many units long the object is.
5. Measure the object.
6. Repeat with other objects.

Object	Unit of Measure	Estimate	Actual Measurement

Tip: Be sure your child is aligning the measuring tool properly. Show your child how to use a finger as a marker if he or she needs to move the measuring tool because the object being measured is longer than the tool.

Name _____

Customary Measurement: Length and Temperature

Find a real example of each object. Choose a unit to measure to the nearest inch, foot, or yard. Write your measurement in inches, feet, or yards.

Object	Write the best unit of measure.	Measurement
I. pencil	_____	about _____
2. book	_____	about _____
3. bed	_____	about _____
4. table	_____	about _____

Temperature

Read the thermometer. Write the temperature.

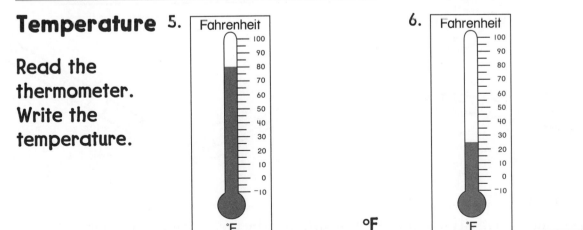

5. Fahrenheit
— 100
— 90
— 80
— 70
— 60
— 50
— 40
— 30
— 20
— 10
— 0
— −10
°F   _____ °F

6. Fahrenheit
— 100
— 90
— 80
— 70
— 60
— 50
— 40
— 30
— 20
— 10
— 0
— −10
°F   _____ °F

Answers: 1.–4. Measurements will vary. For the pencil and book, you might choose inches. For the larger objects, you might choose inches, feet, or yards. **5.** 80°F; **6.** 25°F

Family Involvement Activities   FA89

 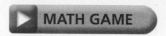

Family Fun — What's My Object?

Use the rulers on page FA91.
Make a chart like the one below for each player.

On Your Own

1. Choose several objects to measure.
2. Write the name of each object on your chart.
3. Measure each object. Write the measurements on your chart. Be sure to include the unit of measure. Do not let other players see your chart.

Together

4. Take turns giving measurement clues about one of your objects. For example, say: "I am thinking of something that is about 4 inches long."
5. Use the inch tape measure to check each object the other players guess.
6. When your object is guessed correctly, measure it again. In the correct row on your chart, write the name of the player who guessed the object.
7. Play until all the objects have been guessed correctly.

My Object	Measurement	Guessed By

Want to do more?

After completing the activity, cut the charts apart. Mix the pieces, and place them face up on a table. Take turns matching the objects to their measurements.

Rulers

Use with pages FA88 and FA90.

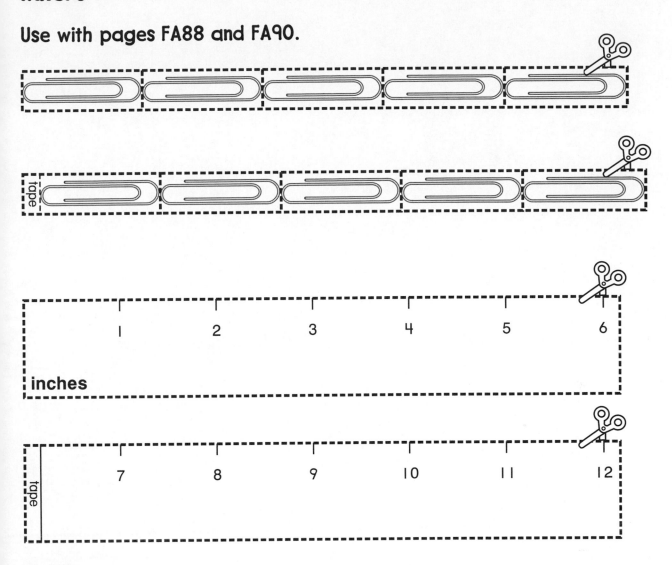

Do This:

Make a paper clip ruler and an inch ruler.

1. Cut out the strips.
2. Place the edge of the first strip on top of the second strip so that it is aligned with the tape mark.
3. Tape.

WHAT WE ARE LEARNING

Customary Measurement:
  Capacity and Weight

VOCABULARY

Here are the vocabulary
words we use in class:

	Cup
	Pint
	Quart
	Gallon

Ounce A unit of weight for
smaller objects

Pound A unit of weight for
larger objects

Name _____

Date _____

Dear Family,

Your child is studying capacity and weight. Here is a
summary of class discussions on these topics.

Capacity

Capacity tells how much something holds. We use
cups, pints, quarts, and gallons as we estimate,
measure, and describe capacity.

Weight

Weight tells how heavy something is.
We use ounces and pounds to estimate, measure, and
describe weight.

Help your child use the activity that follows to practice
using measurement tools and terms.

Sincerely,

Finding Examples of Capacity, Weight, and Mass

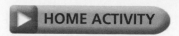

1. To help your child complete the chart on this page, explore food containers in your kitchen.

2. Find at least one example for each unit of measure. Have your child draw and label a picture to show the item. For example, for pounds, your child might draw a bag of sugar and label it "sugar, 5 pounds."

Unit of Measure	Examples
cup	
pint	
quart	
gallon	
ounce	
pound	

Name _____

Customary Measurement: Capacity and Weight

Draw lines to match each container with the amount it can hold.

1.   •   • About 1 pint

2.  •   • About 2 gallons

3.  •   • About 1 gallon

4.  •   • About 1 cup

---

Draw lines to match each object with its weight or mass.

5.  •   • About 1 pound

6.   •   • About 5 pounds

7.   •   • About 2 ounces

8.  •   • About 8 ounces

Answers: 1. about 1 cup; **2.** about 2 gallons; **3.** about 1 pint; **4.** about 1 gallon; **5.** about 2 ounces; **6.** about 1 pound; **7.** about 8 ounces; **8.** about 5 pounds

Family Involvement Activities   FA95

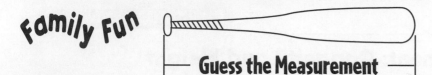

Family Fun

Guess the Measurement

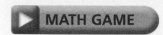

Play a guessing game with the whole family.

1. Display an everyday object, such as a skillet, a phone book, or a melon.

2. Pose a measurement question, for example, "About how much does the skillet weigh?" or "About how long is the skillet handle?" or "About how many cups of water does the skillet hold?" Your question may depend on whether you have a scale, ruler, or measuring cup in your home.

3. After all family members have had a chance to give an estimate, measure the object and announce who had the closest estimate.

4. The winner gets to display an object, pose a question, and determine the next winner.

5. Use the table below to keep track of the actual measurements from each round. Use the measurements as benchmarks for estimating the measurements of other objects. For example, knowing that a skillet weighs two pounds can help you estimate the weight of objects that feel heavier or lighter than the skillet.

Object	Measurement

WHAT WE ARE LEARNING

Metric Measurement

VOCABULARY

Centimeter A unit to measure short lengths
Your child's finger is about 1 centimeter wide.

Meter A unit to measure longer lengths
Your child's arms can spread about 1 meter wide.

Milliliter A small unit to measure how much a container holds

Liter A larger unit to measure how much a container holds

Gram A small unit to measure how heavy an object is

Kilogram A larger unit to measure how heavy an object is

Name _____

Date _____

Dear Family,

Your child is learning about metric units of length, capacity, mass, and temperature.

Length

A centimeter is shorter than an inch. Centimeters are useful for measuring shorter objects, such as kitchen tiles, potholders, and shoelaces.

A meter is a little longer than a yard. Meters are useful for measuring longer objects, such as playing fields and building heights.

Capacity

In grocery stores, you can find beverages in liter bottles. A liter beverage bottle is a good point of reference when discussing liters with your child.

A milliliter is less than a liter. An eyedropper holds about a milliliter of water. You can use milliliters to decide how much glue you need to build a model airplane or how much oil it takes to lubricate your bicycle.

Mass

A paper clip has a mass of about one gram. You can use grams to measure the mass of fresh herbs that go into your favorite sauce.

A house cat has a mass of about one kilogram. You can measure the daily amount of food a tiger eats in kilograms.

Temperature

At 0° Celsius water freezes. At 40°C it is a hot day.

Sincerely,

Get to 20 Centimeters

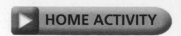

I. Make a centimeter ruler.
Cut out the strips below.
Tape or glue the strips together.

2. Take turns.
The first person looks for an object that measures about 1 centimeter.

3. The next person looks for an object that measures about 2 centimeters.

4. Continue taking turns, each time looking for an object that measures about 1 centimeter more than the previous object.

5. Try to get to 20 centimeters without skipping any steps.

> Remember that there may be more than one way to measure an object using centimeters. For example, you can measure a book's thickness, as well as its height and width.

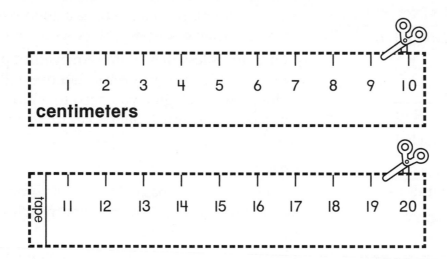

Name _____

Metric Measurement

Measure to the nearest centimeter.

1.
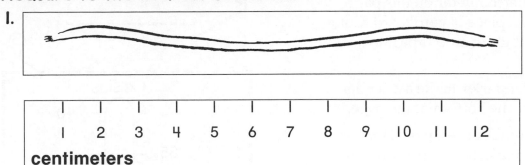

1	2	3	4	5	6	7	8	9	10	11	12

centimeters

Measure about_____ centimeters

Circle the unit that you would use to measure.

2.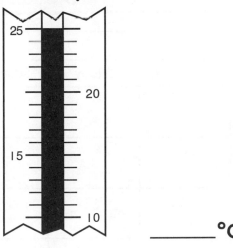

liter

milliliter

3.

liter

milliliter

Circle the unit that you would use to measure.

4.

gram

kilogram

5.

gram

kilogram

Read the thermometer.
Write the temperature.

6.

_____ °C

7.

_____ °C

Family Fun

Tracking the Temperature

MATH GAME

1. Cut out the thermometer on this page and glue it to a piece of cardboard. Color the arrow. Cut it out, and tape it to a paper clip.

2. Use a real calendar or make a calendar like the one at the bottom of the page.

3. Estimate the outdoor temperature. Use the arrow to mark the temperature on the thermometer.

4. Listen to the radio or TV, or check the newspaper to find out the actual temperature. Move the arrow to show it.

5. What type of clothes should you wear today, based on the temperature? Why is it important to consider more than just the temperature when deciding what to wear?

6. Record the temperature on the calendar each day. At the end of each week, talk about the temperature. How did it change over time? Did it get warmer or colder? Did it stay about the same? What predictions can you make about the temperature for next week?

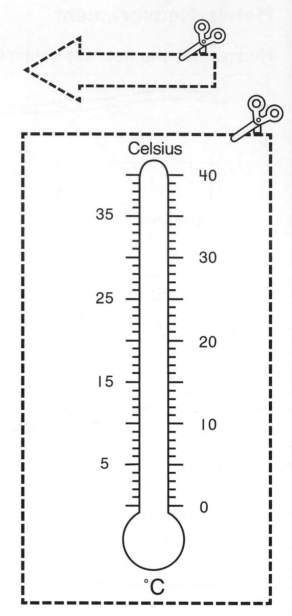

Month						
Sunday	Monday	Tuesday	Wednesday	Thursday	Friday	Saturday

VOCABULARY

Here are the vocabulary
words we use in class:

Perimeter   The distance
around a figure

Area   The number of units
needed to cover a flat
surface

Volume   The amount of
space a solid figure takes up

Name

Date

Dear Family,

Your child is learning how to measure perimeter, area,
and volume.

Perimeter

To find the perimeter of a figure, your child measures
each side with a ruler and adds the measurements.

Talk about times when you needed to find a perimeter.
For example, you might find a perimeter to determine
the amount of trim needed to go around a pillow, the
amount of fencing needed to go around a garden, or
how many rolls of wallpaper border are needed to go
around a room.

Area

To find area, your child counts the number of square
tiles that cover a figure.

Look around your home for objects that are covered
with squares, and have your child help you count the
units (squares) to find the area. Some examples of
objects covered with squares are checker boards, tile
floors or walls, and checkered tablecloths.

Volume

To find volume, your child estimates and then counts
the number of cubes that make up a solid figure.

Work together on the activity that follows to practice
measurement.

Sincerely,

Figures That Figure

I. The side of each square below is 1 centimeter long.
   Draw a figure on the grid.
   Count and add to find its perimeter.

2. Take turns drawing different figures that have the same perimeter.

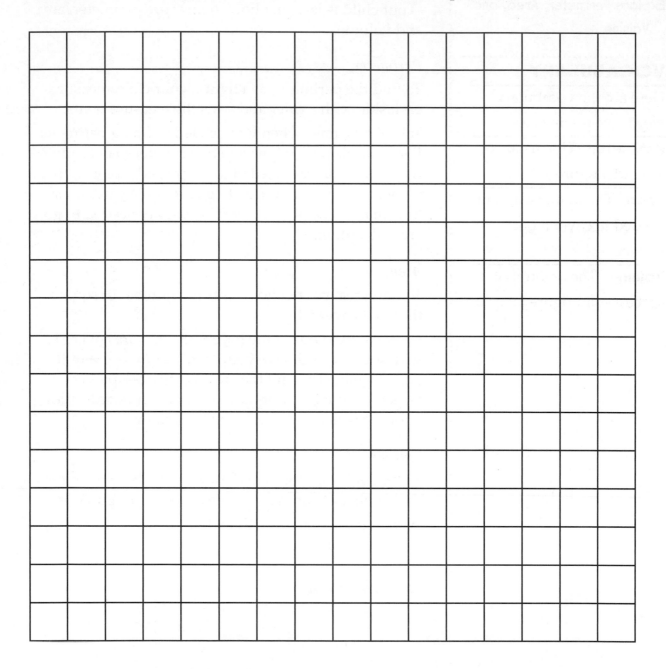

Name _____

Explore Perimeter, Area, and Volume

Add to find the perimeter.

1.

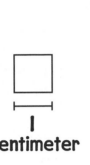

1
centimeter

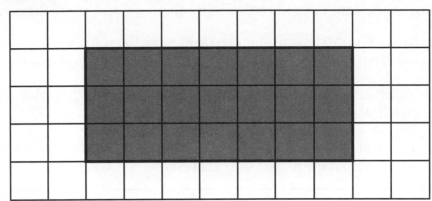

_____ + _____ + _____ + _____ = _____ centimeters

Find the area of the figure.

2.

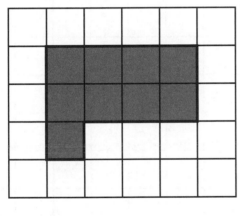

_____ units

3.

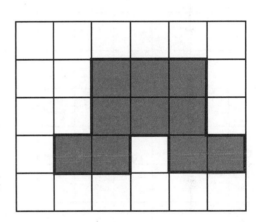

_____ units

Count to find the volume.

4.

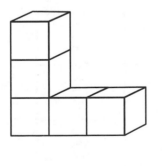

_____ cubes

5.

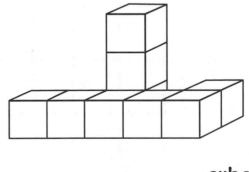

_____ cubes

Answers: 1. 7 + 3 + 7 + 3 = 20; 2. 9 units; 3. 10 units; 4. 5 cubes; 5. 9 cubes

 **Family Fun**

Who Covered the
Greatest Area?

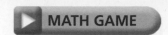

I. Cut out the number cards below. Mix them up and place them face down.

2. Take turns. Choose a number card and read the number. Use one color to shade that many squares. Each player uses a different color.

3. Play continues until everyone has had five turns or until players have shaded all of the squares.

4. Players count the squares they have shaded and compare areas. The player who has shaded the greatest area wins.

1	2	3	4	5
1	2	3	4	5
1	2	3	4	5
1	2	3	4	5

WHAT WE ARE LEARNING

Fractions

VOCABULARY

Here are the vocabulary words we use in class:

Fraction A number that names part of a whole or part of a group, for example, $\frac{1}{4}$

Whole

Equal Parts

This rectangle has 4 equal parts.

Group

One third of the group is gray.

Name _____

Date _____

Dear Family,

Your child is learning about fractions. Here is a summary of our class discussions.

What is a fraction?
A fraction is a number that names part of a whole.

This shape has two equal parts. $\frac{1}{2}$ of this shape is shaded.

What do the numbers in a fraction mean?

The top number tells you how many parts are shaded. 1 part is shaded.

The bottom number tells you how many equal parts are in the whole. There are 4 parts in all.

$\frac{1}{4}$ is shaded.

How do you know which fraction is larger?
You can compare fractions.

This shape has 6 parts. $\frac{1}{6}$ is shaded.

This shape has 3 parts. $\frac{1}{3}$ is shaded. $\frac{1}{3}$ is greater than $\frac{1}{6}$. $\frac{1}{6}$ is less than $\frac{1}{3}$.

When is a fraction equal to 1?

This shape has 4 equal parts.
4 parts are shaded.
The whole shape is shaded.
The fraction for the whole ($\frac{4}{4}$) equals 1.

Help your child use the activity that follows to practice working with fractions.

Sincerely,

Exploring Fractions

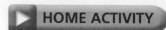

1. Cut out the squares and numbers at the bottom of the page. Keep the shaded square separate.

2. Say a number from 1 to 12. Have your child place that many white squares side-by-side to make a rectangle. Ask, "How many equal parts are there?"

3. Cover one of the white squares with the shaded square, and ask, "What fraction is shaded?"

six equal parts $\frac{1}{6}$

4. Have your child use the numbers you cut out to show the fraction for the shaded part. For example, if you say 6, your child places 6 squares side-by-side and tells you that there are 6 equal parts. As you cover one part with the shaded square, your child tells you that one-sixth is shaded and then uses the numbers to show $\frac{1}{6}$.

My Work Area

Show fraction here.

The top number tells how many parts are shaded.

The bottom number tells how many equal parts are in the whole.

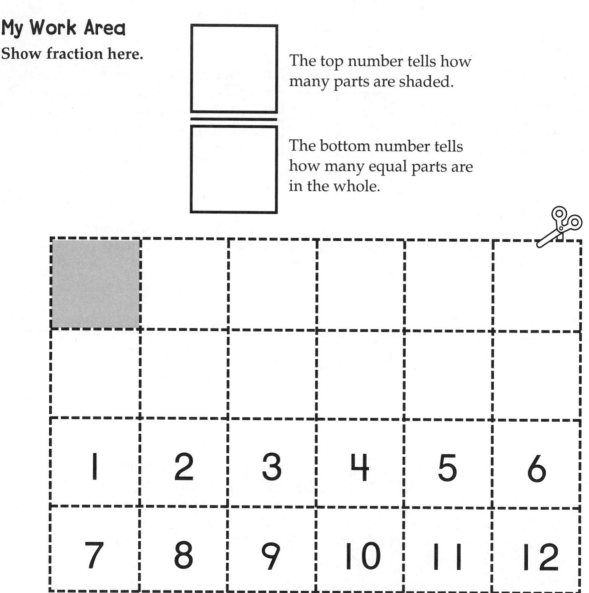

Tip: You might change the activity by using the numbers to make a fraction and having your child use the squares to make a bar that shows the fraction.

Name _____

Fractions

Color one part red. Write the fraction for the red part.

1.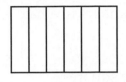

2.

3.

4.

_____   _____   _____   _____

Color to show the fraction.

5. $\dfrac{3}{4}$

6. $\dfrac{1}{2}$

7. $\dfrac{5}{9}$

8. $\dfrac{7}{12}$

Write the fraction for the shaded part.

9.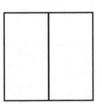

10.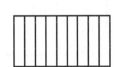

11.

12.

_____   _____   _____   _____

Color one part of each figure. Circle the fraction that is greater.

13.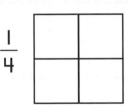

$\dfrac{1}{4}$

$\dfrac{1}{2}$

14.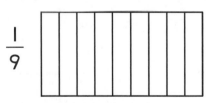

$\dfrac{1}{9}$

$\dfrac{1}{12}$

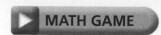
Family Fun   Name That Fraction!

1. Have your child cut out the squares and numbers at the bottom of this page. Keep the shaded squares separate from the white squares.

2. Place the white numbers in a bag labeled *white* and the shaded numbers in a bag labeled *shaded*.

3. Take turns choosing numbers.
   a. Take a number from the white bag and set out that many white squares side-by-side to make a long rectangle.
   b. Take a number from the shaded bag and set that many shaded squares on top of the white squares. **Note:** If the shaded number is larger than the white number, select a new shaded number.

4. Name the fraction that tells about the shaded squares.

5. Write the fraction on paper and draw a picture to show the fraction.

6. Repeat with new numbers. How many fractions can you make?

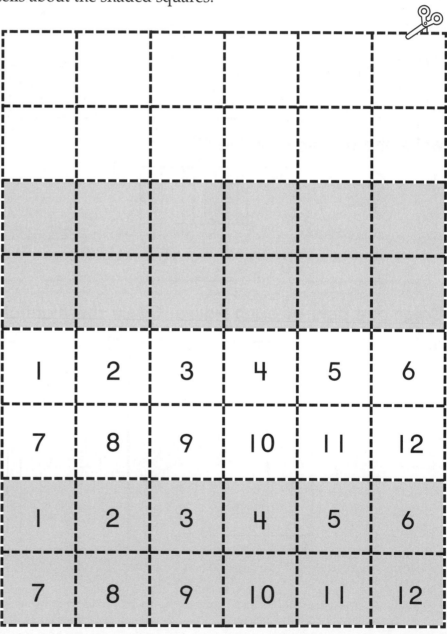

WHAT WE ARE LEARNING

Numbers to 1,000

VOCABULARY

Here are the vocabulary words we use in class:

Hundreds, tens, and ones

The value of digits in 3-digit numbers

Hundreds	Tens	Ones
6	2	5

$$600 + 20 + 5$$
$$625$$

Name _____

Date _____

Dear Family,

Your child is working with numbers to 1,000. In class we are using blocks to model numbers to 1,000. We are practicing reading, writing, and using numbers to 1,000. We are also identifying the place value of digits in a 3-digit number. Here are examples of the work your child is doing in class.

Modeling 3-digit numbers

Show 318 as

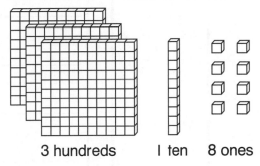

3 hundreds   1 ten   8 ones

Reading and writing 3-digit numbers

Say: Eight hundred fifty-two

Write: 8 hundreds 5 tens 2 ones

          $800 + 50 + 2$

          852

Identify place value in 3-digit numbers

In the number 324

         The digit 3 has a value of 300.
         The digit 2 has a value of 20.
         The digit 4 has a value of 4.

Help your child use the activity that follows to practice reading, writing, and using 3-digit numbers.

Sincerely,

Reading and Writing
3-Digit Numbers

I. Have your child cut out the number boxes at the bottom of the page.

2. Say a number from 100 to 999, and have your child place number boxes on the chart to show the number you said.

3. Have your child say how many hundreds, tens, and ones there are in the number. Then ask him or her to write the number.

hundreds	tens	ones

Our Numbers

_____

_____

_____

_____

_____

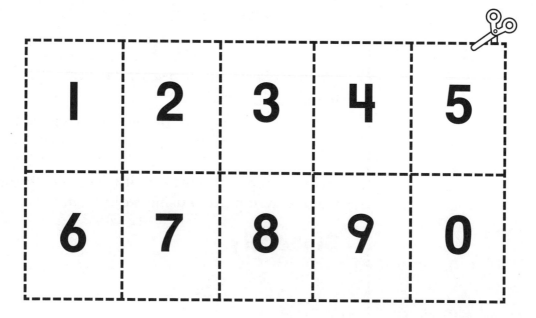

Tip: In the beginning, your child might find it helpful if you place the digits on the chart as you say the 3-digit number. Here are some 3-digit numbers you might say: 147, 256, 381, 405, 592, 638, 713, 824, 967.

Name _____

Numbers to 1,000

Write how many hundreds, tens, and ones.
Then write the number.

1.
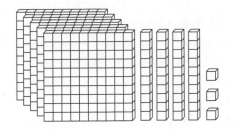

hundreds	tens	ones

_____

2.
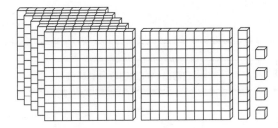

hundreds	tens	ones

_____

3.
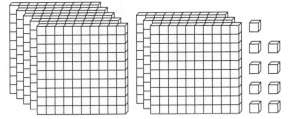

hundreds	tens	ones

_____

Draw lines to match.
Which number has . . .

4. 3 tens •   • 356
5. 3 ones •   • 279
6. 5 ones •   • 861
7. 6 ones •   • 738
8. 5 hundreds •   • 423
9. 9 tens •   • 285
10. 6 hundreds •   • 642
11. 7 tens •   • 514
12. 8 hundreds •   • 997

Answers: 1. 5 hundreds 4 tens 3 ones, 543; **2.** 6 hundreds 1 ten 4 ones, 614; **3.** 8 hundreds 0 tens 9 ones, 809;
4. 738; **5.** 423; **6.** 285; **7.** 356; **8.** 514; **9.** 997; **10.** 642; **11.** 279; **12.** 861

Family Fun   Place-Value BINGO

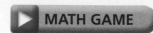

1. Cut out the Bingo grids on this page for each player.
2. Have players write these numbers in random order on their grids: 923, 464, 179, 741, 852, 318, 586, 295, 637, 123, 654, 879, 485, 842, 527, 919. Players' grids should not be exactly alike.
3. Cut out the statements on page FA113, and place them in a bag.
4. Read the statements one at a time, and set them aside.
5. Players cover the square that has the number that matches the statement. If they use pennies to cover their squares, the grids can be reused. When all statements have been read, put them back in the bag and begin again.
6. Tell players to call out "Place-Value Bingo!" when they have covered four squares vertically, horizontally, or diagonally.

Place-Value Bingo!			

Place-Value Bingo!			

Place-Value Bingo!			

Place-Value Bingo!			

Place-Value Statements

This number has 3 ones.	You can say this number as 2 hundreds 9 tens 5 ones.
This number has 6 tens.	This number has 3 tens.
You can say this number as 1 hundred 7 tens 9 ones.	This number has 1 hundred.
This number has 7 hundreds.	This number has 4 ones.
This number has 5 tens.	This number has 7 tens.
This number has 3 hundreds.	This number has 6 ones.
You can say this number as 4 hundreds 8 tens and 5 ones.	You can say this number as 5 hundreds 2 tens 7 ones.
You can say this number as 8 hundreds 4 tens 2 ones.	You can say this number as 9 hundreds 1 ten 9 ones.

WHAT WE ARE LEARNING

Comparing and Ordering
Greater Numbers

VOCABULARY

Here are the vocabulary
words we use in class:

**Greater than >, less
than <, and equal to =**
Symbols used to compare
two numbers

For example:

354 > 345

354 is greater than 345.

679 < 680

679 is less than 680.

425 = 425

425 is equal to 425.

Skip-Count To count
by a given number

For example:

Count by threes.
560, 563, 566, 569

Name _____

Date _____

Dear Family,

Your child is comparing and ordering greater
numbers. Here is a summary of our class discussions.

Compare two 3-digit numbers

Compare 327 and 372.

First: Compare the hundreds. Both numbers have 3 hundreds.

Next: Compare the tens. 327 has 2 tens. 372 has 7 tens.
     2 tens < 7 tens (2 tens is less than 7 tens.)
     7 tens > 2 tens (7 tens is greater than 2 tens.)
     327 < 372 (327 is less than 372.)
     372 > 327 (372 is greater than 327.)

Compare 425 and 423.

If the hundreds and the tens are the same, then compare the ones.
     425 has 5 ones. 423 has 3 ones.
     5 ones > 3 ones (5 ones is greater than 3 ones.)
     425 > 423 (425 is greater than 423.)

Use a number line to put numbers in order

Put 629, 630, and 628 in order.

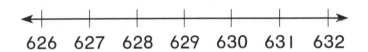

626   627   628   629   630   631   632

Use different ways to skip-count

Count by twos.
252, 254, 256, 258, 260, 262, 264, 266

Count by fives.
415, 420, 425, 430, 435, 440, 445, 450

With your child, do the activity that follows to practice
comparing and ordering greater numbers.

Sincerely,

Comparing Numbers

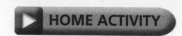

1. Write the following numbers on small squares of paper: 136, 138, 279, 281, 359, 360, 468, 472, 565, 568, 695, 710, 714, 823, 829, 946, 947, and 980.

2. Put the slips of paper in a container, such as a shoe box.

3. Have your child choose two numbers.

4. Ask him or her to place the numbers in the squares below to show which number is greater than (>) the other. Then have him or her change the order to show which number is less than (<) the other.

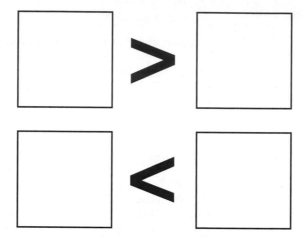

Ordering Numbers

1. Have your child fill in the missing numbers on the number line.

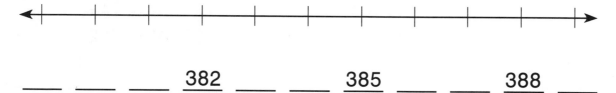

___ ___ ___ 382 ___ ___ 385 ___ ___ 388 ___

2. Now have your child write these numbers in order from least to greatest. He or she can use the number line for help.

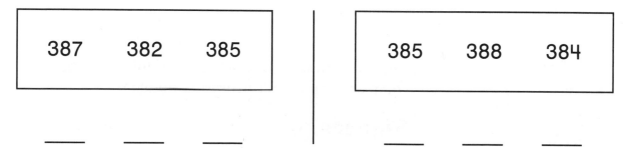

| 387   382   385 | | 385   388   384 |

___ ___ ___   ___ ___ ___

Name _____

Comparing and Ordering Greater Numbers

Write greater than, less than, or equal to.

1. 155 is _____ 145

2. 780 is _____ 870

3. 220 is _____ 220

4. 499 is _____ 399

5. 42 is _____ 420

6. 320 is _____ 302

Compare numbers. Write >, <, or =.

7. 536 ◯ 436

8. 274 ◯ 474

9. 368 ◯ 348

10. 689 ◯ 689

11. 267 ◯ 297

12. 533 ◯ 531

Skip-count by tens. Write the missing numbers.

13. 855, 865, 875, _____, _____, _____, _____, 925

Skip-count by twos. Write the missing numbers.

14. 324, 326, 328, _____, _____, _____, _____, 338

**Use the number line to help you write the numbers
in order from the least to the greatest.**

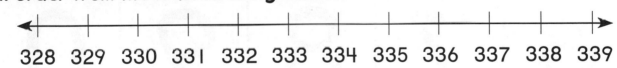

328 329 330 331 332 333 334 335 336 337 338 339

15.

| 335 | 329 | 333 |

16.

| 334 | 328 | 336 |

_____, _____, _____

_____, _____, _____

Family Fun ORDER IT!

1. Have your child cut out the number cards at the bottom of the page, and place them in a bag.

2. Have each player select three numbers from the bag.
   Note: If there are more than three players, make a second set of number cards like the ones at the bottom of the page.

3. Tell each player to use his or her cards to make as many 3-digit numbers as possible. For example: If you select the number cards 2, 7, and 8, you can make these 3-digit numbers: 278, 287, 728, 782, 827, 872.

4. Tell players to write the 3-digit numbers on slips of paper as they make them.

5. After each player makes at least four 3-digit numbers, have him or her arrange the numbers in order from least to greatest.

6. Tell players to check each other's work.

7. Repeat by returning the number cards to the bag and selecting three new cards.

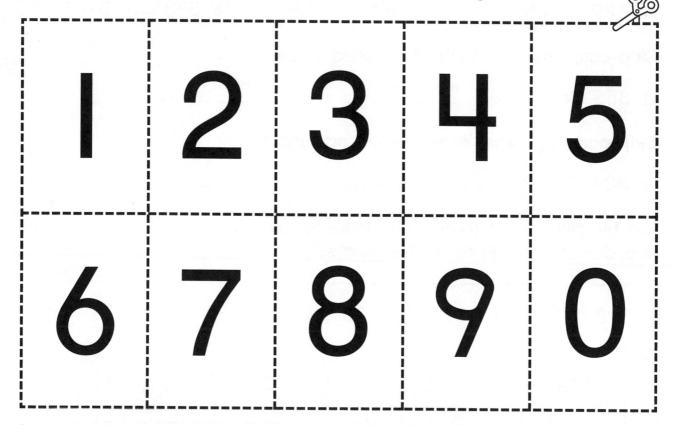

Want to do more? After all players have made 3-digit numbers and placed them in order, place all players' numbers in order from least to greatest. Players take turns placing their slips of paper in a row to show the order. Players may have to move slips of paper as they place new numbers.

WHAT WE ARE LEARNING

Adding and Subtracting
   3-Digit Numbers

VOCABULARY

Here is the vocabulary word
we use in class:

Regroup To exchange
1 ten for 10 ones,
1 hundred for 10 tens
and so on.

Name _____

Date

Dear Family,

Your child is adding and subtracting three-digit
numbers.

Add hundreds

$$\begin{array}{r} 400 \\ + 200 \\ \hline 600 \end{array}$$

Think about facts you know: $4 + 2 = 6$.
Think: 4 hundreds + 2 hundreds = 6 hundreds.

Add 3-digit numbers, with regrouping

hundreds	tens	ones
	[1]	[1]
5	6	7
+ 2	5	5
8	2	2

- Add the ones: $7 + 5 = 12$.
  Regroup 12 ones as 1 ten and 2 ones.
  Write 2 to show how many ones there are.
- Add the tens: 1 ten + 6 tens + 5 tens = 12 tens.
  Regroup 12 tens as 1 hundred and 2 tens.
  Write 2 to show how many tens there are.

  Add the hundreds: 1 hundred + 5 hundreds
  + 2 hundreds.

Subtract hundreds

$$\begin{array}{r} 500 \\ - 200 \\ \hline 300 \end{array}$$

Think about facts you know: $5 - 2 = 3$.
Think: 5 hundreds − 2 hundreds = 3 hundreds.

Subtract 3-digit numbers with regrouping

hundreds	tens	ones
	[7]	[14]
8	8̸	4̸
− 2	5	5
6	2	9

- Look at the ones. Should you regroup?
  Regroup 1 ten as 10 ones.
  Write 7 to show how many tens.
  Write 14 to show how many ones.
  Subtract $14 - 5 = 9$.
- Subtract the tens: 7 tens − 5 tens = 2 tens
- Subtract the hundreds:
  8 hundreds − 2 hundreds = 6 hundreds.

Help your child use the activity that follows to practice
adding and subtracting 3-digit numbers.

Sincerely,

Model Adding 3-Digit Numbers

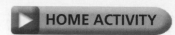

1. Have your child cut out the modeling dot blocks on page FA123.

2. Write 3-digit addition problems on slips of paper, and place them in a small bag. See *Tip* below for suggested 3-digit addition problems.

3. Ask your child to choose a slip of paper. Help him or her use the dot blocks to model the numbers in the problem.

4. Have your child write and solve the problem and tell if he or she needed to regroup.

5. Repeat with other 3-digit addition problems.

My Work Area		
hundreds	tens	ones

Tip: Here are some addition problems that cover the concepts taught in the chapter. Problems with no regrouping: 425 + 132, 735 + 261, 386 + 403; Regrouping ones as tens: 168 + 427, 539 + 233, 625 + 247; Regrouping tens as hundreds: 356 + 192, 641 + 273, 584 + 363. Regrouping ones and tens: 267 + 358, 493 + 128, 576 + 259.

Answers: no regrouping: 557, 996, 789; regrouping tens: 595, 772, 872; regrouping hundreds: 548, 914, 947; regrouping tens and hundreds: 625, 621, 835

Name _____

Adding and Subtracting 3-Digit Numbers

Add hundreds.

1.
```
  4 hundreds      400
+ 3 hundreds    + 300
```

2.
```
  7 hundreds      700
+ 1 hundred     + 100
```

Add.
You may use the dot blocks on page FA123 to show the problems.

3.

hundreds	tens	ones
☐	☐	
4	2	9
+ 1	3	7

4.

hundreds	tens	ones
☐	☐	
5	8	3
+ 2	4	5

Subtract hundreds.

5.
```
  4 hundreds      400
- 3 hundreds    - 300
```

6.
```
  6 hundreds      600
- 2 hundreds    - 200
```

Subtract.
You may use the dot blocks on page FA123 to show the problems.

7.

hundreds	tens	ones
	☐	☐
4	9	2
- 1	3	7

8.

hundreds	tens	ones
	☐	☐
5	3	8
- 2	4	5

Answers: 1. 7 hundreds, 700; **2.** 8 hundreds, 800; **3.** 566; **4.** 828; **5.** 1 hundred, 100; **6.** 4 hundreds, 400; **7.** 355;

Family Fun

Run the Bases!

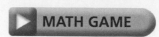
1. Label four paper cups *first base, second base, third base, home plate.*

2. Write the 3-digit numbers listed in the chart on slips of paper. Then place the slips into the paper cups, according to each row of the chart.

first base	254	463	387	576
second base	438	254	625	516
third base	672	457	345	281
home plate	617	536	382	764

3. Have the first "batter" place a game marker, such as a coin, in the batter's box and then select a slip of paper from the *first base* cup.

4. Tell the player to use the number on first base and the number on the slip of paper to write a subtraction problem.

5. The batter solves the subtraction problem, regrouping as needed. All players check the answer.

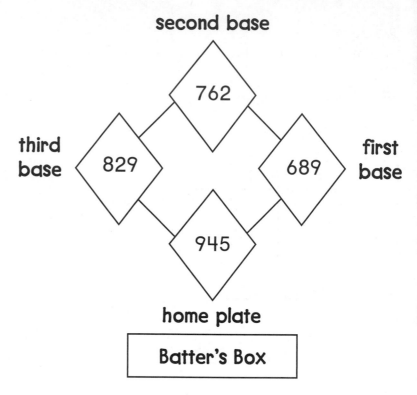

6. If the answer is correct, the batter moves his or her marker to first base. He or she continues "running the bases" by using the number on the base and on a slip of paper from the cup to write and solve a subtraction problem.

7. When any answer is not correct, the player removes his or her marker from the board, and it is the next player's turn.

Want to do more?

Write new 3-digit numbers on slips of paper and add them to the cups. Be sure each number you write can be subtracted from the number on the base.

Answers: first base: 689 − 254 = 435, 689 − 463 = 226, 689 − 387 = 302, 689 − 576 = 113; **second base:** 762 − 438 = 324, 762 − 254 = 508, 762 − 625 = 137, 762 − 516 = 246; **third base:** 829 − 672 = 157, 829 − 457 = 372, 829 − 345 = 484, 829 − 281 = 548; **home plate:** 945 − 617 = 328, 945 − 536 = 409, 945 − 382 = 563, 945 − 764 = 181

Modeling Dot Blocks

Use with pages FA120 and FA121.

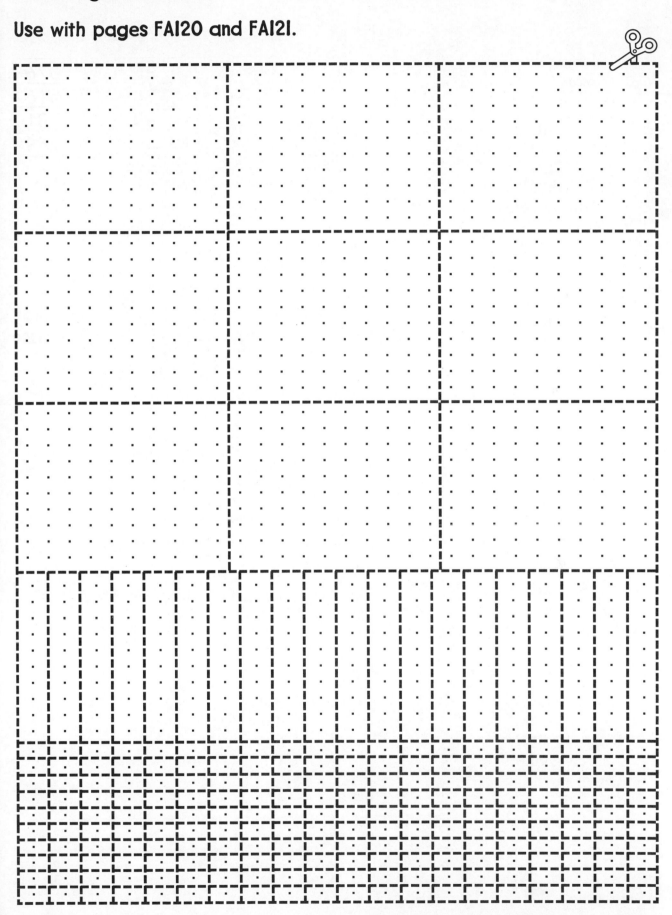

WHAT WE ARE LEARNING

Multiplication and Division
   Concepts

VOCABULARY

Here are the vocabulary words we use in class:

Multiply To combine equal groups to find how many in all

Product The answer to a multiplication problem

$$3 \times 5 = 15$$
↑
product

Multiplication sentence

A number sentence that gives the total for a number of equal groups and the number in each group

$4 \times 3 = 12$ is a multiplication sentence.

Divide To separate into equal groups

$$8 \div 4 = 2$$

Name _____

Date _____

Dear Family,

Your child is learning about multiplication and division. Here is a summary of what our class is learning.

Relate addition and multiplication

$4 + 4 + 4 = 12$ You can add 3 groups of 4. The sum is 12.

$3 \times 4 = 12$ You can multiply 3 groups of 4. The product is 12.

Model arrays

You can make an array to show multiplication. This array shows 3×5. There are 3 rows. There are 5 dots in each row. There are 15 dots in all.

Equal groups

To divide a group of objects into smaller, equal groups, place objects one at a time into each group.

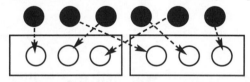

$6 \div 2 = 3$, which means 6 objects, divided into 2 equal groups will have 3 objects in each group.

Dividing with remainders

Sometimes you have objects left over after sharing equally.

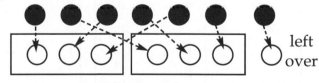
left over

$7 \div 2 = 3$ with 1 left over, which means 7 objects divided into 2 equal groups will have 3 objects in each group AND 1 object left over.

Help your child use the activity that follows to practice multiplication and division.

Sincerely,

Making Equal Groups

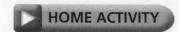

I. Gather 30 small objects that are all alike, such as coins or dry beans.

2. Say a number from 10 to 30 and have your child count out that number of objects.

3. Have your child use the objects to make equal groups in the Work Areas below. Have your child tell the information for each section of the Work Area verbally so that the Work Area can be reused.

4. After your child completes section 2, say a new number from 10 to 30, and have your child repeat the activity.

My Work Area

① I have _____. I will make 2 equal groups.

_____ in each group

_____ left over

② I have _____. I will make 3 equal groups.

_____ in each group

_____ left over

Tip: You can help your child explore making 4 or 5 equal groups by making a work area similar to the one on this page. On a sheet of paper, draw 4 boxes for making 4 equal groups and 5 boxes for making 5 equal groups.

FA126   Family Involvement Activities

Name _____

Multiplication and Division Concepts

Add to find the sum.
Multiply to find the product.

1. $5 + 5 + 5 + 5 =$ ____

2. $10 + 10 + 10 =$ ____

   $4 \times 5 =$ ____

   $3 \times 10 =$ ____

Write the product. Write the related multiplication sentence.
You may draw an array on a separate piece of paper to help.

3. $6 \times 2 =$ ____

4. $3 \times 5 =$ ____

5. $7 \times 4 =$ ____

____ $\times$ ____ $=$ ____

____ $\times$ ____ $=$ ____

____ $\times$ ____ $=$ ____

Draw to show equal groups. Write how many there are.

6. You have 10 .
   Make 3 equal groups.

   [ ] in each group

   [ ] left over

_____

7. You have 12 .
   Make 4 equal groups.

   [ ] in each group

   [ ] left over

Family Fun

Decorate the Apple Tree

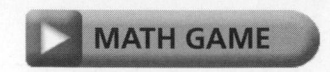

I. Use apples to show each division fact on page FA129.

    a. Cut out the apples on page FA129.

    b. Read the first division fact: 8 ÷ 2 = ☐. Count out 8 apples.

    c. Make equal groups by placing 2 apples in each group on the tree.

    d. Place leftover apples, if any, on the ground under the tree.

    e. Complete the division sentence.

2. Repeat for each fact.

Want to do more?

After showing all the division facts, choose one. Paste it on the tree trunk, and paste the apples on the tree to show the fact.

Answer: 8 ÷ 2 = 4; 6 ÷ 3 = 2; 16 ÷ 4 = 4; 9 ÷ 3 = 3; 15 ÷ 5 = 3; 18 ÷ 2 = 9; 10 ÷ 5 = 2; 18 ÷ 6 = 3; 14 ÷ 3 = 4 with 2 left over; 12 ÷ 6 = 2; 16 ÷ 8 = 2; 20 ÷ 3 = 6 with 2 left over; 24 ÷ 4 = 6; 30 ÷ 3 = 10; 12 ÷ 5 = 2 with 2 left over; 9 ÷ 42 with 1 left over; 25 ÷ 5 = 5; 10 ÷ 3 = 9 with 1 left over; 16 ÷ 3 = 5 with 1 left over; 18 ÷ 5 = 3 with 3 left over; 21 ÷ 7 = 3; 10 ÷ 4 = 2 with 2 left over.

Division facts:
Use with page FAI28.

8 ÷ 2 = ☐	10 ÷ 5 = ☐	24 ÷ 4 = ☐	25 ÷ 5 = ☐
6 ÷ 3 = ☐	18 ÷ 6 = ☐	20 ÷ 3 = ☐	10 ÷ 3 = ☐
16 ÷ 4 = ☐	14 ÷ 3 = ☐	12 ÷ 5 = ☐	16 ÷ 3 = ☐
9 ÷ 3 = ☐	12 ÷ 6 = ☐	9 ÷ 4 = ☐	21 ÷ 7 = ☐
15 ÷ 5 = ☐	16 ÷ 8 = ☐	18 ÷ 5 = ☐	10 ÷ 4 = ☐